ARAB WAR LORDS AND IRAQI STARGAZERS

This edition is dedicated to Judy Rich Lauder

ARAB WAR LORDS AND IRAQI STARGAZERS

Gertrude Bell's
The Arab of Mesopotamia

Second Edition

With an introduction by
Paul Rich

Authors Choice Press
San Jose New York Lincoln Shanghai

Arab War Lords and Iraqi Stargazers
Gertrude Bell's
The Arab of Mesopotamia

Authors Choice Press
an imprint of iUniverse.com, Inc.

For information address:
iUniverse.com, Inc.
5220 S 16th, Ste. 200
Lincoln, NE 68512
www.iuniverse.com

Originally published by Allborough

ISBN: 0-595-14944-8

Printed in the United States of America

MIDDLE EAST CLASSICS

With introductions by Paul Rich

In the wake of recent troubles in the Gulf, an understanding of the area's convoluted history has become invaluable for those who wish to assess the present situation. Many of the border conflicts and disputes concerning the legitimacy of the ruling families and governments have their foundation in the period during and immediately after the First World War. The effects of the British Empire's involvement in the area were widespread, causing cultural and political upheavals that are still at the heart of the area's problems. The iUniverse.com Middle East Classics provide remarkable insight into the events of that period by presenting firsthand accounts of the Gulf at that time, from a variety of authors and viewpoints. Long since out of print and unavailable even to the most ardent enthusiast, these valuable texts are now republished with explanatory introductions by Paul Rich. As a result, the books now once more provide both essential reference material for the Middle East specialist and enlightened reading for those wishing to learn more about the history of one of the world's most dangerous flashpoints.

The Middle East Classics series includes:

VOL I **IRAQ AND IMPERIALISM**: Thomas Lyell's *The Ins and Outs of Mesopotamia*

VOL II **A SOLDIER IN KURDISTAN**: Rupert Hay's *Two Years in Kurdistan*

VOL III **A VOYAGE IN THE GULF**: C. M. Cursetjee's *The Land of the Date*

VOL IV **WARTIME IN BAGHDAD 1917**: Eleanor Egan's *War in the Cradle of the World*

VOL V **CHAOS IN IRAQ**: Aylmer Haldane's *The Insurrection in Mesopotamia, 1920*

VOL VI **THE IRAQI MIND**: Henry Foster's *The Making of Modern Iraq*

VOL VII **ARAB WAR LORDS AND IRAQI STARGAZERS**: Gertrude Bell's *The Secret Basra Papers*

VOL VIII **IRAQ, IRAN AND RITUAL MURDER**: T. C. Fowle's *Travels in the Middle East*

Paul Rich is a Harvard graduate (BA *cum laude* and Ed.M.) who received his Ph.D. from the University of Western Australia, where he was an honorary Research Fellow. He is a Fellow of the American Academy of Political and Social Science and reviews for the Academy's *Annals*. His bibliographical interests include membership of the Rare Books Group of the American Library Association, the Association of College and Research Libraries, and the Independent Librarians' Round Table, as well as the Association for the Bibliography of History. Involved for a decade in education and administration in Saudi Arabia and Qatar, Dr Rich has a particular interest in the historiography of the Arab shaikhdoms. He is the author of *The Invasions of the Gulf*, also published by iUniverse.com

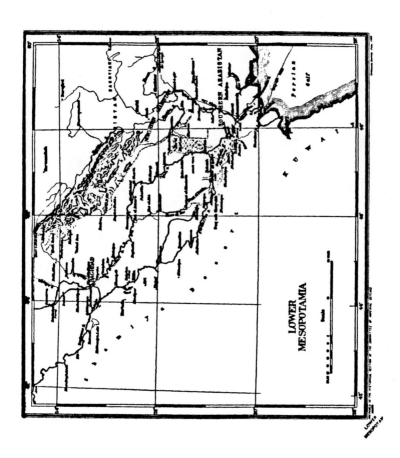

LOWER
MESOPOTAMIA

Scale

General Allenby

Gertrude Bell's *The Arab of Mesopotamia*

Introduction by Paul Rich

"In March [1916] arrived Miss Gertrude Bell, on what was originally intended to be a flying visit from India on her way back to Cairo, where she had been attached to the Intelligence Branch. It was her destiny from the moment of her arrival, until her death in Baghdad ten years later, to devote the whole of her extraordinary talents and unbounded energies to the service of successive administration in Mesopotamia. It was not long before it became clear to her, and to General Head-quarters, Basra, that her peculiar talents could be used to greater advantage as a member of Sir Percy Cox's staff, and in July she was formally attached to the Political Department." - Sir Arnold Wilson, *Loyalties: Mesopotamia 1914-1917*, 1930

"The refinements of this hierachial order, the groupings and classifications," it was noted, "proliferate to the point of Gilbertian incredibility..." - John Bradley, *Lady Curzon's India: Letters of a Vicereine*, 1985

"There is an almost palpable reluctance in the West to face squarely the likelihood that the Arab oil states, alone or in company with their fellow members of OPEC, will again attempt to constrict or curtail the flow of oil to the Western industrial nations and Japan. There is an even greater reluctance to consider the possibility that the West might be forced as a consequence to take active measures to secure its sources of supply in Arabia and the Gulf." - J.B.Kelly, *Arabia, The Gulf and the West*, 1980

Arguably the modern destiny of what was Turkish Arabia or Mesopotamia and is now Iraq, was settled in discussions that took place during 1916 and 1917 in the port of Basra at the head of the Gulf. The headquarters responsible for administering to the areas of the Ottoman province occupied by the British military forces was temporarily located there. (See map *Lower Mesopotamia*.)

The hothouse of visionaries who assembled during that long winter has not received the attention that it deserves. Gertrude Bell's little known *The Arab of Mesopotamia* summons up memories of momentous events in Iraq's second city, euphoniously dubbed the "Marseilles of the East" and the "City of Sinbad", and famous for the export of liquorice-root, dates, malaria, and cholera. The book provides a convenient focus for considering the attitude of the unique cabal to which she belonged.

The Gulf and Iraq have only recently come into the historical spotlight. During World War I this region was overshadowed by the "Last Crusade" in Western Arabia and Palestine - a campaign which attracted avid public attention not only because of the dashing demeanour of Lawrence but also of the heroic bearing of General Sir Edmund Allenby, "a modern Richard the Lionheart" who was described by Field-Marshal Viscount Wavell as "the best British general of the Great War". (See *The Conqueror of Palestine*.) The luckless British commanders of the so-called Forgotten Army in the Mesopotamian campaigns presented scant competition for such stars.[1]

The Arab of Mesopotamia was produced as an instruction manual for neophyte British officers being funneled through Basra as the contest against the Turks brought more and more men to the Middle East.[2] It was formally issued in a more permanent bound form in late 1917 together with a pamphlet about the Ottoman Empire which

Gertrude Bell

Bell wrote in June and July 1917 when the headquarters of the command had moved to Baghdad. In respects a sophisticated propaganda exercise, the book propounded a justification for the Mesopotamian campaign and was produced by the Government Printer in Basra in handy pocket-sized format.

At the time of publication, it was supposedly by an anonymous author. However, until T.E.Lawrence was promoted to fame by the American journalist Lowell Thomas, Gertrude Bell (1868-1926) was possibly the most famous British personality in the Middle East. Charles de Gaury, who served in the Gulf in intelligence and as an Indian Political Service agent, described his first meeting with her:

> She was noticeably thin, and when she rose held herself very erect. Her seeming angularity was accentuated by an unusually long, thin, straight nose, of the kind traditionally held to show unusual intelligence. Her hair, of a sandish-gold colour fading to grey... arranged in the Edwardian style, coiffed up straight from the forehead. Her evening dress was made of cream lace, heavily flounced, and she wore with it a muslin shawl. She was credited with getting her hats, dresses and parasols from Paris, then considered ultra-mondaine for an Englishwoman in the East. The manner of her reception was only just not proconsular.[3] (See *Gertrude Bell*.)

Born to great luxury, the grandaughter of the iron and steel magnate Sir Lowthian Bell, Miss Bell was prepared at the exclusive Queen's College in London, ironically founded for raising the educational level of governesses but long a school for finishing upper class girls in a manner that governesses could not hope for. She then went up to Oxford's Lady Margaret Hall and became the first woman to obtain an Oxford first class in modern history. The years between 1888 and 1915 were spent in alpine climbing, energetic travel and well-financed excavations.[4] H.V.Winstone writes:

As Gertrude travelled in and around that fertile crescent which sweeps from the Nile to the confluence of the Tigris and Euphrates, she became ever more familiar with a group of fellow countrymen who shared with her the means to travel at leisure and who were drawn, much as she, by archaeological discovery and the infinite mysteries of deserts and forbidden cities.[5]

The connections forged during these adventures were of tremendous importance to her emerging career in the land of the Arabs. Associates from this period included D.G.Hogarth, T.E.Lawrence ("a pleasant boy" she thought, when she met him on a dig at Jerabalus in 1911), Percy Cox, and other Middle East luminaries. She became part of an urbane inner circle:

> Not for nothing was...D.G.Hogarth, author of the famous account of the exploration of Arabia aptly titled *The Penetration of Arabia* (1904) made the head of the Arab Bureau in Cairo during World War I. And neither was it by accident that men and women like Gertrude Bell, T.E.Lawrence, and St.John Philby, Oriental experts, all posted to the Orient as agents of empire, friends of the Orient, formulators of policy alternatives because of their intimate and expert knowledge of the Orient and of Orientals. They formed a "band" - as Lawrence called it once - bound together by contradictory notions and personal similarities: great individuality, sympathy and intutitive identification with the Orient, a jealously preserved sense of personal mission in the Orient, cultivated eccentricity, a final disapproval of the Orient.[6]

CAPT. W. H. I. SHAKESPEAR, C I E
Indian Political Dept.
Killed in action in Arabia, Jan. 1915

CAPT R L BIRDWOOD, C I E
Indian Political Dept
Killed in action, 17th Nov. 1914

Summoned to Cairo

In November 1915 Bell's tremendous experience in the Middle East and knowledge of its languages resulted in a summons to Cairo where she was attached to the Arab Bureau, a "think tank" *cum* propaganda machine and intelligence operation godfathered by Sir Mark Sykes, a hybrid which never fitted into the ordinary military command structure.[7] The Bureau was understandably interested in what was going on in the Gulf, a guarded bailiwick of the Indian Political Service. Bell's visit (early 1916) to the Viceroy of India, Lord Hardinge of Penshurst, resulted in her being posted to Basra in 1916 to mediate between Cairo and the Indian Political Service officers who were administering occupied Iraq. Relying on the old friendship with the Viceroy which dated from their youth, she was able to overcome his suspicion that Cairo sought to meddle in what he regarded as a strictly Indian sphere of influence.[8] (He had become quite hawkish about the war and was urging that the forces push on to Baghdad.)

The deaths of a number of popular and prominent Indian Political Service officers in the initial stages of the Mesopotamian campaign contributed to the Government of India resolution to keep the Gulf as a part of its fief. Casualties had included Captain R.L.Birdwood (of a famous Anglo-Indian family, he died in the very first Gulf battle of Fao on 17 November 1914), and Captain W.H.I.Shakespear, considered one of the most brilliant of the Political Department's young men (killed in what is now Saudi Arabia in January 1915). (See *Portraits* opposite.)

Whenever the question of ultimate control of the Mesopotamian theatre was raised, proponents were quick to invoke the sacrifice which these fatalities represented. Hardinge wrote to General Wingate (November 1915) to protest "the surrender of all the advantages for which India has been fighting in Mesopotamia during the past year and the creation of an Arab state lying aside our interests in the Persian Gulf, which would mean commercial ruin for many of our undertakings, and probably chaos in those provinces."[9]

Although initially viewed with suspicion on her arrival in Basra, Bell's talents were quickly recognised and she was made Oriental Secretary on the staff of the High Commissioner for Iraq, Sir Percy Cox.[10] A prodigious writer and correspondent, her presence on the Commission for Iraq signalled a much enhanced historical record of British activities in Basra and Baghdad. (See *Landing the English Mails at Basrah*.) The American missionary the Reverend John Van Ess composed a *little ditty* about her voluminous reports:

> G is for Gertrude, of the Arabs she's Queen,
> And that's why they call her Om el Mumineen,
> If she gets to heaven (I'm sure I'll be there!)
> She'll ask even Allah 'What's your tribe, and where?'[11]

While much of her best work appeared in the secret intelligence communiqués of the Arab Bureau, enough of what she wrote was publically circulated in her lifetime such that there was no doubt about her literary ability. Three of her books are in Allborough editions. *The Letters of Gertrude Bell* (first published in 1927) appears as *Gertrude Bell on Baghdad and the World: A Very Private Correspondence* in the Allborough Collector's Library series. *Persian Pictures* (1928) is, appropriately, the first volume in the Allborough Middle East Editions, retitled *Shadows of Death in Iran: Mists in a Mysterious Land*.

However, the long-term consequences of her advice while serving as confidant and adviser in Basra and Baghdad are more open to question than is her facility as a writer. The forcefulness of her presence is never questioned. She arrived in Basra in March 1916 just before one of the greatest British military disasters of World War I, the entrapment of Sir Charles Townshend's forces at the Iraqi city of Kut. Townshend had surrendered to the Turks on April 29th, 1916 following a series of misfortunes that had put British control of the entire region into question. Arguably, the British never recovered from their loss of composure in Iraq. The circumstances favoured someone like

LANDING THE ENGLISH MAILS AT BASRAH.

Gertrude Bell who had firm ideas about what should be done in Iraq at a time when others had only doubts.

Following the British reoccupation of Kut (February 1917) and of Baghdad (March 1917), Bell and the other headquarters staff moved to Baghdad. The civil administration and its planning during this period was in the hands of Cox and his long-time second-in-command, Sir Arnold Wilson, who tangled with Bell on many occasions. Wilson got little chance to perform on his own, only becoming Acting Civil Commissioner of Mesopotamia in April 1918 when Cox became British Minister in Tehran, and then becoming Officiating Resident in 1920.[12] (See *Sir Percy Cox*.)

In the view of St.John Philby (also a member of the Basra office), the relationship between the two men did Wilson little good.[13] It is not necessary to resort to the services of a psycho-historian to speculate about the effect on Wilson of being in Cox's shadow for so many years. In any case, he was not an imaginative person and when there were no precedents for the Iraqi situation, the solutions he tried were unsuccessful. Some felt he was a caricature of Colonel Blimp, "an arch-imperialist... repressive...".[14] Bell thought he was "a very remarkable creature"[15] and Philby complained that he delivered monologues which sounded as if he had swatted them in the Encyclopaedia Britannica.[16] Philby wrote of Wilson:

> His Latin tags in the Political Office and the Mess, sometimes misquoted, and his super-patriotism - Cromwell's "We are a people with the stamp of God upon us" was his favourite quotation - became something of a joke. Yet he was without a shadow of doubt, the hero-figure of the young Political Officers who came to Iraq after the war."[17]

The incompatibility between Wilson and Philby was one reason why Philby left the Indian services and went to work with the Ibn Saud.[18]

The Indian Politicals, who had long enjoyed control of the Gulf sheikhdoms, were insistent on controlling the British interests in Mesopotamia. Furthermore, they believed in a permanent British suzerainty, regardless of what promises about post-war plans had been made to the Arabs. Thus, the death of IPS comrades made this an almost sacred subject with Wilson, reinforced by the fact that the majority of the troops (and casualties) were Indian Army.[19] Bell managed to accommodate this for the time being, while hanging onto her Cairo connection and lobbying for more subtle schemes of indirect rule that Wilson could not appreciate.

An Edwardian Lady and Edwardian Gentlemen

Gertrude Bell's success in carving out a place for herself in the administration of Iraq owed a great deal to her social position. As H.V.Winstone notes, she was gifted at hobnobbing with the élite. On one occasion she revealingly wrote: "I really think I am beginning to get hold of the women here, I mean the women of the better classes. *Pas sans peine*, though they meet one more than half way...I am now going to try a more ambitious scheme and get the leading ladies to form a committee to collect among rich families (themselves) funds for a small women's hospital for the better classes, about which some of them seem keen."[20] She sought to assign the Arabs to positions in the same tables of precedence as she did the British, and she enthusiastically supported the creation of an Iraqi monarchy.

This might not have totally surprised the sheikhs, who had long noted the way in which IPS officers were immersed in a miasma of protocol and were often men for whom "reality was the tribalism within the cloisters".[21] The penalty for such delusions was further emphasis of already existing social divisions. Surveying British intervention in what was to become Iraq, it is difficult to not recall J.A.Hobson's opinion in *Imperialism* that the penalty of imperialism is preordained.[22] The priorities of the British government went beyond the setting up of desert democracies.

x

MAJ.-GEN. SIR PERCY Z. COX
G.C.M.G., G.C.I.E., K.C.S.I., D.C.L.
Indian Political Dept

Gertrude Bell was accepted *despite being a woman* because of her secure place in the Establishment. She had the same retrorse prejudices as Cox and Wilson.[23] The group that gathered in Basra was as Imperial in mien as any that the British Empire could muster.[24] Wilson's biographer, John Marlowe, remarked: "There was something in his 'credo' to repel almost everyone."[25] While Iraq, small in population, could hardly display the full arcana of Imperial trappings and was not a tapis upon which the IPS could weave the intricate patterns of India, the British Empire managed to successfully impose its patterns wherever it went - and the attempt was made at a *mysterium magnum* in Basra and Baghdad no less than it was it was elsewhere.

Cox and Wilson's in part in these designs reflected the greater ambitions they cherished for the establishment of a Middle East Empire to rival the Indian version. They were obsessed with the idea of an Imperial civil service that would include Arabia, Iraq, the Trans-Jordan, and even the Sudan. This was light years away from Arab tribal concerns and only a handful of the Arab leaders heard the trumpets. While it has been made out that the Arabs were staunch allies in the war, the truth is that they had serious misgivings about the defeat of the Turks at the hands of the British - doubts which were confirmed as the evidence pointing to the development of a long-term British presence accumulated.

Gertrude and the Forty Thieves

In March 1921 Winston Churchill called a conference of forty Middle East experts in Cairo to decide upon the post World War I power divisions in the Middle East. Bell was there, along with Churchill, Cox and T.E.Lawrence. The arrangements were more calculated to please British taxpayers than Arab nationalists, and did not grant the Arabs their much longed for independence. On the contrary, surrogate monarchies were established in Trans-Jordan and

Iraq, and the British imposed a long, unproductive interregum in the Middle East.

The immediate post-war years were disastrous on a personal level for some of those present - in particular for Arnold Wilson. He had been mesmerized into thinking the Middle East could be controlled by a neo-Imperialist mishmash of moral influence and ceremony. It couldn't, and when he replaced Cox in Iraq in 1918, he soon lost his superiors' confidence.[26] Arnold Toybee called his aggrandized dreams "incredible" and Lord Curzon, no introvert when it came to Imperial expansion, had to admit that Wilson's proposals were "rather remarkable". Perhaps the height of the absurd was reached when Wilson supported the expulsion from primary school of twenty boys in Mosul for wearing "Arab" colours. He unconvincingly argued that if they were allowed to wear the scarves that they wished, that the consequence would be race riots.[27]

When insurrection or civil war occurred in Iraq in 1920 (viewed later by some Iraqis as a war of independence) Wilson was unable to handle the "strange" problems of nationalism. He resigned in October 1920 to become British Petroleum Company representative in the Gulf. Bell now seemed to have granted her wish of a free hand in a British-sponsored kingdom where she would occupy the seat nearest the throne. By the time of her death, however, the pipe-dream had receded. The Middle Eastern dreampalace as a *quid pro quo* for IPS lives sacrificed was never realised. Such policies can be explained if not exonerated, but they left multitudinous problems for future generations.

This is not of course to discount the more crass explaination of events in Iraq: oil. John Strachey writes:

> The fact that, in the late eighteenth and early nineteenth centuries, the British Government in India had acquired, for strategic reasons, the overlordship of South Persia and of the Sheikhdoms round the Persian Gulf, greatly assisted the early British oil prospectors, when they established the Anglo-Persian Oil Company in the first decade of

the twentieth century... It was no accident that the main share went to British rather than to French or Italian companies. Here was a genuine example of the acquisition of political sovereignty (*de facto*) actually bringing major economic gain.[28]

However, it would be a mistake to concentrate solely on the oil and to overlook the personal and social motives.[29] In Bell's case these were much stronger than any interest in mineral rights.

Is Iraq a Viable Country?

The soldiers who read Gertrude Bell's book could be pardoned if they thought, on the basis of her explanation, that they were freeing a nation from Turkish oppressors. In actual fact, whether the territory comprising what is now Iraq ever was a nation remains debatable, and equally debatable is whether the British intervention freed anyone, or if, rather, it succeeded in imposing a deeply disliked regime on the indigenous peoples who were given no choice in the matter. In considering the *beau geste* efforts of Bell, Wilson, Cox and their confrères, it would perhaps be wrong to apply the modern standards of Amnesty International and United Nations resolutions on human rights. Nevertheless, Mesopotamia's Shia majority and numerous minorities were trodden over in creating a dynasty which had its firmest supporters in suppliants and sycophants.

Had a republic been created - which was favoured by some British such as St.John Philby - Iraq still may not have had enough reason to be a country. Arnold Wilson wrote in *Mesopotamia 1917-1920* that "...the idea of 'Iraq as an independent nation had scarcely taken shape, for the country lacked homogeneity, whether geographical, economical or social."[30] On the other side of the coin is the complicated question of the viability of dividing a region into minute areas in order to placate racial and religious groups. It becomes increasingly apparent - in the wake of the breakup of the Soviet Union and of Yugoslavia - that limits of one kind or another must exist to these divisions and subdivisions, precisely in order to promote stability within the factions.

In the case of Iraq, perhaps a reasonable compromise would have been to honour the Ottoman boundaries; to allow the Kurds, Armenians, and Assyrians a separate Mosul state; and to provide small Sunni and Shia states based respectively on Baghdad and Basrah.[31] For all of Bell's knowledge and Cox's accumen and Wilson's sagacity, the solution which did emerge of importing a king and of creating a throne had the marks of an impatient quick fix for a centuries-old problem. Moreover, this solution was not arrived at out of concern for the newly-minted Iraqi people but rather with the objective of maintaining Britain's stature and power in the area.[32] Parallels have been drawn with recent American intrusions in Vietnam and the Middle East, calling into question whether United States policy was anything but self-serving:

> Then, as if ruled by inexorable laws, history repeated itself for the United States. The British dilemma of the 1920s became the American dilemma... British efforts to resolve this dilemma presaged with uncanny precision what the United States did half a century later in Vietnam, as in the Middle East, to arrest its own decline.[33]

A British decline was in evidence in the aftermath of World War I. Britain was exhausted, as demonstrated by its inability to adequately garrison the Middle East. Dame Freya Stark wrote:

> The old order goes. Like the country squire in England, the sheikh is becoming an anachronism; the Latin centralizing conception is ousting the old personal ideas which were common to our Teutonic forefathers and to the bedouin of the desert... we were fundamentally in agreement with the old order: the differences between the feudalism of the East and that our public schools and universities

was not so great as one might think: and there were many points of contact between a tribal chieftain and the sons of English country gentlemen who ran the Empire.[34]

Pace gentlewomen such as Bell.

A Chastising Experience

While a number of extraordinary women have roamed the Middle East, taking advantage of a chivalrous attitude towards their sex as protection against brigands and despots, Gertrude Bell alone managed to achieve a high official position. Major J.T.Gorman, the prolific author of juvenile adventure tales, wrote a story about Lydia Staunton, the daughter of a fictional Sir Thomas Staunton of the Indian Politicals. Living in Sheikh Othman in Aden, Lydia manages all the adventures that would of been expected of boys in Henty-style novels and admits that, "I get very sick of being a girl myself, and I try to forget it as much as I possibly can." (See *Lydia Staunton escaping the Bedouin Raiders*.) Gertrude Bell had the opportunity to live out adventures quite as colourful as anything that Major Gorman ever imagined for Lydia.

Edward Said remarks: "The British agent-Orientalist - Lawrence, Bell, Philby, Storrs, Hogarth - during and after World War I took over both the rôle of expert-adventurer-eccentric (created in the nineteenth century by Lane, Burton, Hester Stanhope) and the rôle of colonial authority, whose position is in a central place next to the indigenous ruler: Lawrence with the Hashimites, Philby with the house of Saud, are the two best-known instances."[35] He might well have added Bell and the Iraqi monarchy to the list.

However, Bell's influence at the Iraqi royal court - a court which she had helped create - declined in the period 1922-26. Moody and mercurial, she had thrived on the attention that previously had been paid her and was depressed by what she perceived as a loss in stature.[36]

She died mysteriously from an overdose of barbituates in July 1926. H.V.F.Winstone tactfully comments: "Many who were in Baghdad at the time believed that she committed suicide, but the medical report and the findings of an inquiry appointed by the High Commissioner were never put on public record."[37]

After Bell's death, Iraq continued to be a bitter and chastising experience for Whitehall policy makes, pursued by commitments which were impossible to fully honour. The British involvement in the region was immense and the resources scant. Palestine and the Suez Canal competed with Aden and Cyprus for troops, and one small undertaking such as Cyprus easily could have absorbed the entire year's overseas development budget: "Even a heap of rocks with the grandiose title of the Kuria Muria Isles, located a few miles off the coast of Oman had been bequeathed to Queen Victoria, and had therefore to be defended, in theory if not in practice."[38]

The 1920s and 1930s were a time of "quiet instability" in Iraq.[39] During endemic political turmoil and tribal revolt, accompanied by chronic financial crisis, it would have been unreasonable to expect anything remarkable in the way of social, economic or administrative progress.[40] Iraq remained an important British military staging post and its airfields (at Habbaniya, Baghdad, Basra, Mosul, Shaibah, Seram adia) were presumed upon well into the post World War II era, although the reluctant Iraqis were anything but perfect hosts. The implicit *threat* of British air power continued until the withdrawal of British Forces Gulf and Air Forces Gulf from Bahrain at the end of 1971.[41] The Imperial topee, albeit the worse for wear, retained its symbolic import into the second Elizabethan Age.[42]

The Love-Hate Relationship

As Professor Said suggests in *Orientalism*, there was a love-hate dimension to British relationships with the Middle East, which is discernible in Bell's telling remark in

Lydia Staunton escaping the Bedouin raiders

the *Asiatic Turkey* section of her book (p.124) when she comments, perhaps tongue-in-cheek, about the scholars of Baghdad:

> "And if to the Occidental these authors of many tomes may seem to be linked to fame with ropes of sand, that is not the estimate of their country men. They have influence; their approval is an unquestioned passport in Islam, it will open doors in distant places where mild Learning sits in wrapt self-contemplation, give you the freedom of what the East appreciates as good company, condone your errors and whitewash your crudities."[43]

Iraq did not maintain even briefly the constitutional pose which the British scripted - and given the cynicism of many of the British officers involved in setting up the new state, perhaps that was to be expected. Along with its neighbors it has seldom enjoyed even a brief period of stability. Between Iraq and Syria in the decades since World War II there have been 32 *coups d'état*. Phoney Parliaments and a procession of greedy, thinly disguised dictators testify to the failure of the West to found democratic systems when the opportunity seemed available.[44]

Along with despotism there has been unrelenting persecution of minorities, largely ignored in the West with its amazing lack of understanding of the religious and racial pluralism of the Middle East. Notwithstanding its apology for British invention, Bell's handbook might well be distributed to policymakers of the present era and read profitably by them.[45] Bell herself ponders the dilemma: "True, the Turks were bad masters, but who shall say that the English will in the end be better?" (p.123.) The mounds of prose generated in response to Iraq's 1991 invasion of Kuwait have largely ignored the previous Western incursions into the Gulf - the difficulties of late would have been all too familiar to Bell.[46] Neither naval blockades and the stopping of suspect ships nor hopes of establishing democratic regimes are new themes. January 1991 was not the first time that Western air superiority contributed to a victory in Iraq.

Many motifs used in the coverage of the 1991 Gulf War have a familiar ring. The past in this case is truly a prelude. Russians were a largely impotent but important consideration in British strategic thinking in 1914-18. Kuwait and other Gulf sheikhdoms seemed threatened and the solution was an invasion.

A reading of Bell should arrest any assumption that countries like patients automatically improve with treatment. Not all patients recover: some are terminally ill. *The Arab of Mesopotamia* makes a case: it is up to the reader to decide how well that case is made. Bell appeals to the British sense of responsibility, and to a "trust imposed upon national honour." (p.61) Some would feel that there was an unwarranted audacity to such a claim.[47] If another reason for the stubborn efforts of Bell and others to make Iraq into a nation on *their* model simply was to justify the deaths of friends such as Birdwood and Shakespear, the killing of so many more young men and the destruction of much of Iraq was a peculiar memorial. (See *Ruins of Basra, 21 November 1914*.)

Still, nobody will ever deny that Gertrude Bell was an exceptional woman. In July 1958 the Anglophile Iraqi royal family was brutally murdered by the Iraqi Army, starting the chain of events which brought Saddam Hussein into power. Charles de Gaury, who had known the Hashimite dynasty since the days when he first met Bell in Iraq, arranged a commemoration at the Chapel Royal of the Savoy in London. Authorities had been reluctant to support such a gesture, claiming that it might prejudice future British interests of Iraq. However, the dead king had been a member of the Royal Victorian Order, and so de Gaury was able to obtain the use of the Chapel, the order's official sanctuary. Ushering before the service, he met one very elderly lady at the door who looked familiar. "I am Lady Richmond," she explained, "sister of Gertrude Bell who put Faisal the First on the throne. May I have a seat?"[48] A well located pew was speedily produced. Surely Gertrude Bell would have been gratified.

Ruins of Basra

"In the High Commission the silver plate had been set out again for dinner and the candles were lit. The portraits of Kings, Viceroys, Admirals and Governors loomed from the dark paneling, each meticulously labeled and framed in gold. The two brass cannons on the lawn in front of the portico still pointed outwards as they did for a hundred and fifty years, one over the harbour, the other to the mountains. Because the sun had set the flagstaff was empty. In the huge white drawing-room, sitting separately and in silence...[the Commissioner and his wife] heard through the darkness the sirens of the approaching dictator." - Douglas Hurd, *Truth Game*, 1972

NOTES

1. See David L.Bullock, *Allenby's War: The Palestine-Arabian Campaigns, 1916-1918*, Blandford Press, London, 1988, 7, 151. "All it [the Mesopotamian Army] got was anything that was too old, too worn or too inadequate for use elsewhere; even the ammunition was labelled 'Made in the USA. For practice only'." A.J.Barker, *The Neglected War: Mesopotamia 1914-1918*, Faber and Faber, 1967, 18.

2. "This was published anonymously but Gertrude Bell admits to having written it." Peter Slugett, *Britain in Iraq, 1914-1932*, for Middle East Centre, St Antony's College, Oxford, by Ithaca Press, London, 1976, 340. Winstone lists the title in the bibliography of *Gertrude Bell* with the date 1918. The British Library catalog does not list a copy, but the Library of Congress does. There is no reference to the book in most bibliographies of the Middle East, nor does it appear in *Bookman's Price Index*, vols. 37-43. It is not in Stephen Longrigg's exhaustive Royal Institute of International Affairs publication *Iraq, 1900 to 1950*. Probably it ranks in rarity with the 1940 Golden Cockerel Press edi-

tion of Bell's *The Arab War - Confidential Information for GHQ Cairo from Gertrude L. Bell.*

3. Gerald de Gaury, *Three Kings in Baghdad, 1921-1958*, Hutchinson, London, 1961, 44.

4. See H.V.F.Winstone *Gertrude Bell*, Quartet Books, New York, 1978, esp.23, 95, 127, and *passim*.

5. *Ibid.*, 110.

6. Edward Said, *Orientalism*, Routledge & Kegan Paul, London
and Henley, 1978, 224.

7. See Winstone, *Gertrude Bell*, 163.

8. H.V.F.Winstone, *The Illicit Adventure: The Story of Political and Military Intelligence in the Middle East from 1898 to 1926*, Jonathan Cape, 1982, 205-6. See the portrait of Hardinge in my book *Elixir of Empire*, Regency, London, 1989, 20.

9. qtd.Winstone, *Gertrude Bell*, 171. See *Ibid.*, 172-73.

10. The uninspired life of Bell by W.D.Hogarth in the *Dictionary of National Biography* is of limited use except for a chronology. For a recent appreciation of her career as archaeologist and museum curator see Brian Fagan, "Bell of Baghdad", *Archaeology*, Vol.44, No.4, July/August 1991, 12-16.

11. Winstone, *Gertrude Bell*, 182.

12. See Keith Jeffrey, *The British Army and the Crisis of Empire, 1918-22*, Manchester University Press, 1984, 147. Although often strained, Bell's relationship with Wilson also was marked by appreciation. In May of 1920 she wrote, "A.T.has been given a K.C.I.E. - I'm very very glad. He well deserves it and I'm so specially glad of the recogni-

tion of his work by H.M.G. ...." Lady Bell (Mrs.Hugh) with Lady Elsa Richmond, *Letters of Gertrude Bell*, Vol.II, Ernest Benn, London, 1927, 488. Wilson approvingly included Bell's memorandum "Self-Determination in Mesopotamia" in his opus *Mesopotamia 1917-1920: A Clash of Loyalties* (Oxford University Press, 1931) although a remark (p.275, footnote) perhaps indicates just why they were often as dagger points - when criticising General Aylmer Haldane for his handling of the Iraqi insurrection in June 1920, Wilson mentions that Haldane cited as evidence for his own views a private letter from Bell: "..it was, to say ths least, imprudent to prefer her private miscalculations to the measured misgivings, amply supported by reports from all centres, of her official superior." Bell seemed oblivious to the effect of dashing off letters that circumvented Wilson.

13. See "Introduction", H.St.John Philby, *The Queen of Sheba*, Quartet Books, 1981, 18.

14. Peter Mansfield, *The Arabs*, Allen Lane, 1977, 216.

15. *Ibid.*, 203.

16. *Ibid.*, 207.

17. *Ibid.*, 214.

18. Briton Cooper Busch, *Britain, India, and the Arabs, 1914-1921*, University of California Press, Berkeley, 1971, 249.

19. One influential paper, the *Statist* was particularly shrill in advocating the use of non-white troops. See Norman Etherington, *Theories of Imperialism: War, Conquest and Capital*, Croom Helm, London 1984, 56 n.23.

20. Winstone, *Gertrude Bell*, 219.

21. See Roy Foster, "Oh, Jolly Good!", *Times Educational Supplement*, 22 November 1985, 25.

22. "Imperialism is a depraved choice of national life, imposed by self-seeking interests which appeal to the lusts of quantitive acquisititiveness and of forceful domination surviving in a nation from early centuries of animal struggle for existence. Its adoption as a policy implies a deliberate renunciation of the cultivation of the higher inner qualities which for an individual constitutes the ascendency of reason over brute impulse. It is the besetting sin of all successful States, and its penalty is unalterable in the order of nature." J.A.Hobson, *Imperialism*, University of Michigan Press, 1965 [1902], 368.

23. "The real trouble as Hobson saw it was that the imperialists - well organised in small but interlocking groups, wielding influence not in political theory only but in social life, in short, in the public schools, in the cadet forces, in the scouting movement, in the Press, in the pulpit - believed in what they said and in what they were doing, and he knew he could not convince them by any words or by any pages of closely-reasoned argument that 'every enlargement of pages of closely-reasoned argument that Great Britain in the tropics is a distinct enfeeblement'." A.P.Thornton, *The Imperial Idea and Its Enemies: A Study in British Power*, 2nd ed., Macmillan, 1985 [1959], 73.

24. "Arnold Wilson, schooled in the Indian Army and then the Political Service in India, Persia and Mesopotamia, became, as a member of Parliament in the 1930s, a notable public patriot, Milnerite and Miltonic, yet an Erastian Anglican, a dedicated Imperialist, strongly averse to Continental entanglements. He was an advocate of concentrated national authority in all spheres, of national self-sufficiency, of a National Political party, of compulsory National Service and of national insurance and welfare -- to improve the human resources of the young *patria* which he considered he knew at firsthand by virtue of the 'Cobbett-like peregrinations and conversations' throughout the country

record in his *Walks and Talks* books." J.H.Grainger, *Patri-otisms: Britain 1900-1939*, Routledge & Kegan Paul, 1986, 355.

25. qtd.*Ibid.*

26. "In theory control of the civil administration was vested in the GOCInC, Mesopotamia, who from May 1919 to January 1920 was Sir George MacMunn. In practice, however, the administration was almost entirely in the hands of Colonel Arnold Wilson, who had been appointed Acting Civil Commissioner in April 1918. Apart from being subordinate to MacMunn (himself subject to War Office in-structions), Wilson also received orders from the Secretary of State of India, 'in matters of policy', and the Indian government 'in certain matters of administration'. In Lon-don, too, the Foreign Office insisted on having a major say in decision-making" Keith Jeffery, *The British Army and the Crisis of Empire, 1918-22*, Manchester University Press, 1984, 147. Wilson was acting Civil Commissioner because Cox was temporarily British Minister in Tehran. *Ibid.* 133-155.

27. See my appreciation of Arnold Wilson in *The Inva-sions of the Gulf*, Allborough, Cambridge, 1991, 234-35.

28. John Strachey, *The End of Empire*, Victor Gollancz, 1959, 158.

29. Cf. *Ibid*

30. Arnold T.Wilson, *Mesopotamia 1917-1920: A Clash of Loyalties*, Oxford University Press, 1931, x. "Separatist tendencies were strong in Basra; it was scarcely to be hoped that the wilayats of Basra and Baghdad could main-tain their existence as an autonomous state without the revue it was hoped might eventually be derived from the economic resources of the Mosul wilayat. Yet three-quar-ters of the inhabitants of the Mosul wilayat were non-Arab,

five-eighths being Kurdish, and one-eighth Christians or Yazadis. The Kurdish problem proved insoluble.*Ibid.*

31. See Philip Marlowe, *The Persian Gulf in the Twentieth Century*, Cresset Press, 1962, 114.

32. See William Stivers, *Supremacy and Oil: Iraq, Turkey, and the Anglo-American World Order, 1918-1930*, Cornell University Press, Ithaca, 1982, 8.

33. *Ibid.* 9.

34. Freya Stark, *The Journey's Echo*, John Murray, London, 1963, 27.

35. Said, *Orientalism*, 246.

36. The alternative moods of elation and depression are obvious in her letters. "Gertrude was always inclined to the use of superlatives - there were no half-tones in her repertoire." H.St.J.B.Philby, *Arabian Days: An Autobiography*, Robert Hale, London, 1948, 131.

37. Winstone, *Illicit Adenture*, 360.

38. David Lee (Air Chief Marshal GBE CB), *Flight from the Middle East: A History of the Royal Air Force in the Arabian Peninsula and Adjacent Territories, 1948-1972*, HMSO, London, 1980, xiii.

39. See *Ibid.*, 3ff.

40. Marlowe, *The Persian Gulf*, 118.

41. See Lee, *Flight from the Middle East*, 31, 34.

42. "In the 1920s and 30s aircrew not only wore flying topees over their normal helmets and goggles in their own cockpits, but were also compelled to wear thickly padded 'spine pads' under their shirts as protection against sun-

stroke. The discomfort of these trappings was intense: the slipstream playing on top of the topee caused the goggles to vibrate and any movement of the head outside the protection of the windscreen allowed the slipstream to get under the brim of the topee, giving the neck a nasty jerk." *Ibid.*, 80.

43. "To soak the heat, sand and discomfort were anathema; they claimed to have hated every moment of it, but curiously enough, proceeded to talk about it with a kind of reluctant nostalgia for the remainder of their lives. The isolation and the vague but irresistible feeling of a link with Biblical times has affected many Britons who have dedicated their lives to serving one or other of the many Arab potentates in some advisory or administrative capacity." *Ibid.*, 90.

44. Pierre Salinger with Eric Laurent, *Secret Dossier:The Hidden Agenda Behind The Gulf War,* Penguin, New York, 1991, 223. Published in French as *Guerre du Golfe: Le Dossier Secret* by "Olivier Orban" and translated into English by Howard Curtis.

45. "The United States side said it was entirely willing to meet our request for an exchange of information concerning the activities of extremist Shia groups in the country and certain States of the Gulf Co-operation Council... We agreed with the American side that it was important to take advantage of the deteriorating economic situation in Iraq in order to put pressure on their country's government to delineate our common border. The Central Intelligence Agency gave us its view of appropriate means of pressure, saying that broad cooperation should be initiated between us, on condition that such activities are co-ordinated at a high level." Brigadier Fahd Ahmad Al Fahd, Director-General of the State Security Department to His Excellency. Sheikh Salem Al Sabah Al Salem Al Sabah, undated but following his visit to the CIS from 12 to 18 November 1989, qtd. Salinder, *Secret Dossier*, 240-41.

46. "The circumstances of the British connection, and the unpopularity of the Mandate, made it inevitable that anti-British fervour should be an obligatory attitude for the constitutional opposition, and also made it inevitable that successive governments, within the limits imposed by the Mandatory relationship and by the assistance which they needed from Great Britain, should view with the opposition in this anti-British fervour as being the only alternative to dictatorship as a means of keeping themselves in office." Marlowe, *The Persian Gulf*, 115.

47. "The unthinking chauvinism which took whole armies of scarcely-bearded youths into the trenches of 1914-18 was, in the end, a terrible blasphemy; we all know that now... If there was a villain it was the curriculum, hidden or not-so-hidden, of the public schools themselves." Nicholas Bagnall, "Thoughts of Mother, Eton and You", *Times Educational Supplement*, 20 March 1987, 24. See George H.Nadel and Perry Curtis, "Introduction", Nadel and Curtis, eds., *Imperialism and Colonialism*, Macmillan, 1964, 1. *Cf*.D.K.Fieldhouse, "Hobson and Economic Imperialism Reconsidered", Robin W.Winks ed., *British Imperialism: Gold, God, Glory*, Rinehart and Winston, New York, 1963, 47.

48. de Gaury, *Three Kings in Baghdad*, 205.

Mesopotamia.

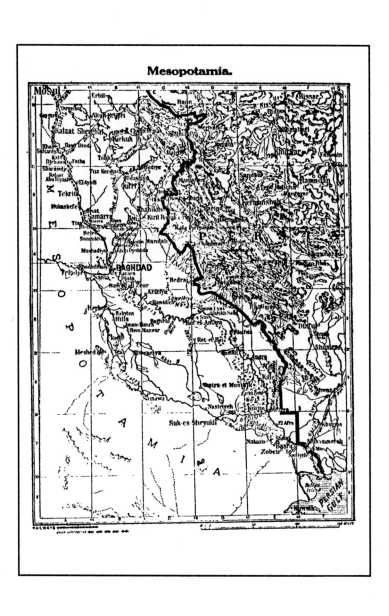

THE ARAB OF MESOPOTAMIA

Price Re. 1.

BASRAH :
PUBLISHED BY THE SUPERINTENDENT,
GOVERNMENT PRESS.

CONTENTS.

PREFACE.

THIS pamphlet consists of a series of brief essays on subjects relating to Mesopotamia, written, during 1916, by persons with special knowledge of the subjects dealt with.

All have already been published in some shape, but it has been suggested that many of those whom the fortune of war has brought to these regions would be glad to have the opportunity of obtaining them in a convenient and permanent form. It is with this object that they have been reprinted and placed on sale.

The Arab of Mesopotamia.

The Arab Tribes of Mesopotamia.

THE cultivated delta watered by the Tigris and
Euphrates is inhabited by Arab tribal confederations, more or less settled, who are immigrants
from the Arabian deserts. Some have been established in Mesopotamia from a remote period,
others have come in during the last two or three
hundred years, but all are originally nomads of
the interior wilderness. The unbroken drift of
her peoples northwards is one of the most important factors in the history of Arabia. The underlying causes were probably complex, but chief
among them must have been a gradual change in
the climatic conditions of the peninsula, involving
slow desiccation, together with the pressure of an
increasing population on a soil growing steadily
poorer. To the hunger-bitten nomad, the rich
pastures of the Syrian frontier, the inexhaustible
fertility of Mesopotamia, offered irresistible
attractions, and opportunities for expansion were
found in the weakness and political exhaustion of
the neighbouring northern states, whether they

were Turkish, Byzantine, Persian or yet earlier empires. The long records of Babylonia enable us to trace the process in its earlier historical phases, a study of existing conditions shows that until a recent period it was still going on, and if a forecast may be hazarded, it will not be arrested in the future, though the nature of the migration may be altered. Instead of devastating hordes, sweeping like locusts over cornfield and pasture, the surplus population of Arabia may find in a Mesopotamia reconstituted by good administration not only abundant means of livelihood but far-reaching possibilities of social and intellectual advance ; and they will be received with welcome in a land of which the unlimited resources can be put to profit in proportion to the labour available.

The conversion of the wandering camel breeder and camel lifter into a cultivator of the soil, in so far as it has taken place in Mesopotamia, was an inevitable process. In their progress northward the tribes found themselves ultimately upon the limits of the desert ; the wide spaces essential to nomadic existence no longer stretched before them, while the pressure of those behind forbade any return. They were obliged to look to agriculture as a means of livelihood. Thereby they

lost caste with the true Badawin, yet, though
these last would scorn to intermarry with tillers
of the earth, shepherds and herdsmen of buffaloes,
they are nevertheless of the same blood and·tra-
dition, and not infrequently fragments of very
ancient and famous Arabian tribes are present
among the cultivators upon the outer limits of
Arabian migration. Thus in Mesopotamia the
Bani Tamim, who are divided among various big
tribal groups, were masters of the whole of Central
Arabia before the time of the Prophet and still
form a large part of the Oasis population—their
first appearance in Mesopotamia dates from about
the beginning of the Mohammedan era ; and the
Khazraj, now found chiefly on the Persian frontier, supplied by their martial exploits in the
southern deserts much of the romantic stock in
trade of the pre-Mohammedan poets.

It follows from the conditions under which
settlement has been effected that the old tribes
are often widely scattered along the edges of the
cultivated land, large units which once ranged
over extensive stretches of desert having been
split up and thurst apart by the intrusion of others.
For example, the Jubur, a tribe now only half
nomadic, are found along the Tigris as far North

as Mosul, as well as on the eastern frontiers, of Syria, and the Zubaid are divided between Mesopotamia and the volcanic districts east of Damascus.

The transition from a nomadic to a settled life is always a slow process and the very doubtful security offered by Turkish administration did not tend to hasten it. Except in the immediate neighbourhood of big towns, such as Baghdad and Basrah, tribal organization has not been relinquished, tribal law and customs hold good and tribal blood feuds continue to be a terrible scourge. A periodical reversion to tents is common and even the reed villagers are semi-nomadic, shifting frequently from place to place. The puzzled mapmaker may find his last addition to geographical knowledge removed, almost before his eyes, from the spot assigned to it in his survey and re-erected on another site. But the rising value of land tends to pin down these restless husbandmen and no sooner do they settle than their numbers increase out of all comparison with those of their hungry if prouder brethren who neither plough nor harvest the wilderness. The Muntafik confederation occupy an area which in round figures extends 65 miles from East to West and 50 miles from North to

South, and number, at a rough estimate, not less than 200,000 souls, whereas the whole of the great Badawin group of the Anazah which peoples the Syrain desert from Aleppo to the sands of Central Arabia, can scarcely be reckoned at a higher figure.

The proximity of Persia and the existence in Mesopotamia of Karbala and Najaf, two of the most holy shrines of the Shiah sect, to which the Persians belong, with the resulting influx of Persian pilgrims, have brought the country much under Persian influences. Nomad Arabia belongs wholly to the Sunni half of Islam, yet the tribes settled in Mesopotamia have embraced, almost without exception, the Shiah faith. These, however, who maintain purely nomadic habits, "people of the Camel" as they proudly call themselves, have kept as a rule to the desert doctrine and are almost invariably Sunni.

From the head of the Persian Gulf up to Qurnah tribal organisation has almost died out, except that many of the peasants working in the date gardens belong to the tribes of our staunch ally on the Persian side of the river, the powerful Shaikh of Mohammarah, who has in the past maintained the right to mobilise them for his own tribal operations. Above Qurnah the country, from Euphrates to Tigris for some distance along the banks of both rivers, is occupied by the Muntafik, a large and loose confederation of tribes of different origin, all of whom acknowledge, to a less degree or a greater, the over-lordship of the Sa'dun clan. These Sa'dun are sprung from a Mecca family closely related to the Sharif, a branch of which migrated to Mesopotamia towards the close of the Abbasid period, about the beginning of the 15th century. Themselves Sunnis and of the purest Sunni stock, they established their authority over the Shiah tribes and played a very considerable part in the stormy history of the land. In the case of one scion of the family who had rendered valuable service in Central Arabia, the Porte even tried the experiment of appointing him Wali of Basrah, but it quickly proved a failure and was abandoned.

Of late years their power as a ruling family has been gradually disintegrating owing to internal rivalries and dissensions and at present, though several of the leading members of the Sa'dun possess large estates in the Basrah Wilayet, they are able to exact but a small portion of their dues from their tribal tenantry and as tribal leaders in the field they are now of little account. Their family prestige is still, however, considerable.

The position of the Sa'dun clan, as affected by the outbreak of war between Turkey and Great Britain, has been a difficult one, for many of them own properties both in the territories in British occupation and in those at present controlled by the Turks ; but except in the case of two or three irreconcilables their behaviour has on the whole been reasonable and intelligible, and there is little doubt that they will all come into the fold when they are satisfied that Turkish rule has vanished for ever from the Basrah Wilayet.

Some part of the Muntafik is still nomadic ; the rest inhabit reed huts, villages, and even towns, cultivate the land and breed sheep, cattle, buffaloes and camels. Many of them who belong to the settled sections roam the desert in spring with their flocks and herds for the sake of pasturage.

The tribes of southern Mesopotamia are better armed than those above Kut and the Muntafik are well provided with modern rifles.

Above them, along the course of the Tigris almost up to Kut, lie two large and powerful tribes ranging from the river to the Persian Hills.

Of these Al Bu Muhammed, a socially inferior and possibly non-Arab people, are rice-growers in the marshes on either side of the Tigris and breed immense herds of buffaloes which are exported in great numbers to Syria. Like all Marsh Arabs they have maintained a semi-independence, and, down to the youngest member of the tribe, they are well armed with rifles. The second big group, that of the Bani Lam, have occupied the country above Amarah for the last four or five hundred years. Their Shaikhs claim descent from a famous pre-Mohammedan tribe of Eastern Arabia, but, in spite of their pretentions, none of the Badawin of the inner desert would regard them as equals or intermarry with them. Their most prominent Shaikh, Ghadhban, a great rebel against the Ottoman Government before the war, joined the Turks against us, but has now reconsidered his position, and most of his house came to terms with us as soon as we advanced up the Tigris. The Bani Lam are cultivators, but none of them have entirely abandoned nomad life. They inhabit tents and are generally on the move with their herds from February to June. Their horses and camels are reckoned the best in Mesopotamia. They are good shots, especially from the saddle.

Round Kut, both on the Tigris and on the upper part of the great Hai canal, which flows out of the river southwards, the Bani Rabi'ah bear sway, a tribe of ancient fame in Arabia. They are a turbulent people, well-known robbers and disturbers of traffic along the river, but not so efficiently armed as their neighbours to the South. Still less well provided with rifles and more submissive to control are the two smaller tribes which cultivate the Tigris banks up to Baghdad, the Toqah and the Zubaid, while the inhabitants of the Euphrates marshes above Nasiriyah, though their reputation leaves much to be desired, have not shown themselves ill disposed towards us.

Far down in the scale of civilization as these amphibious dwellers in swamp and reed bed would seem to be, the amazing quickness of the Arab in adopting himself to new conditions and profiting by unexpected opportunities must never be forgotten. A child born yesterday in a reed hut or a black goat's hair tent may well be found practising medicine or the law in Baghdad before the next quarter of a century is over, and, though his father may prefer to abide by something more nearly resembling the old customs, a solid balance at the bank will testify that he leads the simple life by choice and not of necessity.

The

Basis of Government in Turkish Arabia.

No country which turned to the eye of the world
an appearance of established rule and centralized
Government was to a greater extent than was the
Ottoman Empire a land of make-believe. On
paper every co-efficient of sovereignty, every
process of administration could be found in its
proper place, with its fitting attributes and its
staff, from Pasha to Gendarme, all with suitable
emoluments clearly set down and activities
defined. In due course the satisfactory results
of the exertions of these worthies would be chro-
nicled, the taxes they had collected, the fines
they had exacted, the roads they had drawn
across mountain and desert, the provincial and
municipal labours which they had punctually
performed. On paper; but for the meticulous
inquirer who could carry his researches further
than the written pages, parade the shadowy
personnel, count out the money bags, or journey
along the airy structure of the Sultan's highways,
disillusion was at hand. And he who, without
being guilty of incautious curiosity, was forced

by circumstances to test the relations that existed between documentary evidence à la Turque and the hard facts of the Ottoman Empire, was apt to find himself lost in bewildered annoyance, not unaccompanied by uncontrollable hilarity—annoyance when his progress was brought to a standstill by unbridged torrents or the rifle shots of the local magnate whom paper ordinances were not strong enough to check, hilarity when the neighbouring Wali expatiated to him on the benefits which had resulted to the land from his own forethought (under God) in regard to the adequate provision of bridges, or the Commandant assured him solemnly that every part of the wilderness was covered by the dovelike wings of the Sultan's peace.

That the Turkish Empire should have run at all was, at a hasty appreciation, a matter for marvel, but increased familiarity furnished a clue to a part at least of the problem. It ran not on the paper ordinances, but on unwritten laws, unrecorded provisions of Government, habits of command and of obedience inherited from a remote past and applicable to an immediate present, which was not so very dissimilar from the past ; it was founded not on the power and efficiency of Wali and Commandant, but on the authority of village headman, tribal Shaikh and local Saiyid. Outside the narrow circle of the towns the official mechanism was set aside, while more efficacious if more ancient methods of procedure were adopted, and over a great part of Asiatic Turkey the executive lay in the hands of men who had no part in the make-believe.

But since the final basis of genuine administration was to a large extent independent of Ottoman officials, it will remain undisturbed if from any specified part of the empire those officials should disappear. The power of Shaikh or headman was derived neither from the Sultan nor yet from the Constitution, nor can it fall with them. It is deeply rooted in the daily life of the people, and with wise supervision, will form for several generations to come the staple of law and order. Indeed, it should form the groundwork of all Government until the time when developed facilities of communication and a wider circle of enlightenment shall lead by a natural growth to such measure of centralization as is profitable. It is safe to predict that it will be a centralization very different from that which the Committee of Union and Progress sought to impose upon the inchoate agglomeration of creeds and races which in the course of six years they dragged into two ruinous wars.

The material which lies to the hand of those who may be called upon to undertake the supreme task of creating prosperity in rich lands which have lain derelict for over half a millenium can scarcely be demonstrated more clearly than in the domain of judicial administration. The stock in trade of Turkish Justice, familiar to all residents and to most travellers in the Ottoman Empire, depended ultimately on sacred law, but Turkey had to a certain extent modified her strict adherence to inspired legislation by the superimposition of provisions which were mostly derived from the Code Napoléon. Thus the Criminal Code and the Code of Criminal Procedure in use in Turkish Courts were based on the French, and the Code of Commercial Procedure, which guided the Commercial Courts, had the same origin. Foreigners, however, refused to admit the application of the Commercial Code to themselves, except where issues not above £T10 in value were in question, and for all others where they were concerned the Ordinary Civil Code, the Mujalli, was employed. The Mujalli rests

on Mohammedan religious law, the actual code
having been drawn up by Turkish jurists. All
Turks being Sunnis, and belonging moreover to
the Hanafi sect of that division of Islam, the law
which the jurists followed was that of the Hanafis,
and in consequence the Shiahs (that is to say,
over 90 per cent. of the population of Mesopotamia) together with the members of three other
orthodox Sunni sects outside the Hanafis, Malikis,
Safais and Hanbalis, were obliged to submit to
Hanafi ruling. The Mujalli dealt with suits connected with rents, sales, exchange, contract, evidence and many other matters, but there
remained a large body of civil suits which were
beyond its jurisdiction. All domestic disputes,
marriage, divorce, and every relation between
husband, wife and child, all questions of inheritance, and all land cases were the province of
the Shara' Courts, the Courts of Sacred Law
which were presided over, not by a civil judge
but by a Qadhi. The Shara' law rests on no
formulated Code. *Mutatis mutandis*, it may be
compared to our judge-made law, if it were
understood that whenever the judge was in doubt
he should seek a solution from a passage of the
Old or New Testament. The Shara' depended

on the individual opinion of the Qadhi, or more technically on his individual interpretation of the Quran and the traditions, subject to any knowledge of the interpretation of his predecessors which he might possess.

Such in outline was the structure of Turkish Law, and theoretically all disputes in the Turkish Empire, from those between merchants in Stambul to those between Kurdish chieftains in their mountain fortresses or Arab Shaikhs in their arid deserts, came under its purvue. But the most cursory acquaintance with any province of the Empire disproved the theory. Take, for example, Turkish Arabia : a short experience would convince the observer that the Sultan's writ fell powerless ten hours journey West of Baghdad and possibly after a still less prolonged March to the South of the capital of Iraq, while it was palpably a subject for ridicule two hours South-east of Damascus. Even when gendarmes and police officers were on the spot to emphasize the majesty of the Law, it was not the Courts, Civil, Criminal or Shara', not the judge, nor the Qadhi who regulated the relations between man and man or assigned the penalties for breaches in their observance. Behind all legal paraphernalia lay the old sanctions, understood and respected, because they were the natural outcome of social needs, a true social contract handed down by the wisdom of forbears to descendants who found themselves confronted by problems to which the passage of centuries had brought no modification. Village headman and Arabian Amir "sat in the gate" as the Kings of Babylon and Judæa had sat before them, and judged between their people without code or procedure. The Shaikh in his tent heard the plaint of petitioners seated round his coffee hearth, and gave his verdict with what acumen he might possess, aided by a due regard for tribal custom, calling on the coffee-drinkers to bear witness before God to his adjudication. Or the tribal Saiyid, strong in his reputation for a greater familiarity than that of other men with the revealed ordinances of the Almighty— and yet stronger in the wisdom bought by long experience in arbitration—delivered his awards to all who referred to him. Moreover, the decisions reached were as a rule consonant with natural justice, and invariably conformable to the habits of thought of the disputing parties.

Thus it happened, that in spite of the unrelaxed efforts of Ottoman Officials to drag all cases, more

especially all criminal cases, into their own courts,
beyond the immediate limits of the towns the
bulk of the crimes and misdemeanours of the
nomad and of the settled population, from murder
and robbery under arms to the pettiest disagree-
ments, never reached the Turkish law courts,
afforded no livelihood to professional pleaders and
hired witnesses, nor were subject to the expense
and delay entailed by judicial proceedings. In
their colossal ignorance of the temperament of the
alien races whom they ruled, and in their blind
impulse to draw all authority into a single net,
the Turks not only neglected but actively dis-
couraged the delegation of power, though they
were unable to prevent it. Officially the jurisdiction of an Arab Shaikh was recognised as little as
possible and any Turkish judge would have scorned
to refer to him ; but in practice a weak and inefficient Government allowed him to go his own way,
not only for good but for evil, with occasional
brief efforts to prevent him—efforts which were
applied as impartially to that which was of value
in existing conditions as to that which was
harmful. Their spasmodic character made them
the more irritating to all concerned.

But in the eyes of wiser and more sympathetic

rulers the system of local justice which prevails
over the land will have far more than a sociological
interest. It is not only in itself a strong weapon
on the side of order and good conduct, but it has
induced in the people habits of mind which are of
advantage to the State. Where no adventitious
profits can arise from litigation there is no inducement to excessive litigiousness ; when the procedure is transparently simply the probity of liti-
gants is open to fewer temptations, and in point
of fact the absence of any love of litigation for its
own sake and the honesty of the disputing parties
have already been noticed with commendation by
British Officials in the Iraq who have been engaged in the administration of justice. Not only
is the need of detective work on the part of the
police largely abrogated by the almost disconcert-
ing sincerity with which the accused will own up
to his offence, but the limited facilities for the
pursuit of complex enquiries, as well as for the
execution of sentences possessed by the extem-
porised courts of the village gate and the coffee
hearth have accustomed the people to be satisfied
with primitive expedients. These are no less
effectual while they are far less vexatious than the
exhaustive inquisition and the expensive retribu-

tion of more highly elaborated—let it not be said
necessarily of higher civilizations. On small
issues the evidence of an oath is readily accepted,
especially in the rural districts, and the plaintiff
will go on his way content if the defendant will
swear to his own innocence in terms which are
considered binding. An oath will be taken on the
Quran or on the grave of some holy man of local
celebrity, or even on the holy man in his own
person. " By the life of this Saiyid.......... ! "
and all who hear the words know beyond question
that if the speaker is forsworn his temerity will
bring upon him within the year a judgment
greater and more inexorable than that of man.
In place of litigation resort is made to arbitration
—even the reference to the Shaikh is primarily
of this nature. The judgment delivered by the
arbitrator is accepted by both parties as final, and
is usually the result of a sincere effort to gauge the
facts and to deal fairly between the disputants.

The universal recognition of arbitration as a
sound judicial process has helped to the solution
of what might otherwise have been an awkward
problem in the preliminary organisation of the
occupied territories in the Iraq. In place of the
Shara' Court, which dealt with all the more inti-

mate sides of Mohammedan life, the English judge
calls upon the doctors of Islam to act as arbitra-
tors. Cases which would have come to the Shara'
Courts are now adjudicated by men selected for
their acquaintance with Mohammedan law as laid
down in the holy books, and whereas in Turkish
days none but a Hanafi Qadhi was available,
each division and sect of Islam can now choose
an approved jurist of its own peculiar complexion,
whose judgment when delivered is ratified and
recorded in the British Court.

By the same method, the jurisdiction of the
Shaikh, clearly a notable asset in the administration of districts which are wholly innocent of road
and rail, and characterized either by such super-
fluity of water as makes them unapproachable, or
by such absence of that essential element as forbids
passage across them, can be preserved with a full
regard to the rights of a sovereign Government.

It is obvious that elementary judicial processes
are suited only to a society which is as yet in an
elementary stage of development, but no less
obvious is the converse proposition, though it is
perhaps more difficult to bear in mind. Men
living in tents, or in reed huts almost as nomadic
as the tent itself, men who have never known any
control but the empty fiction of Turkish authority

—for in spite of the assurances of Wali and Commandant, the tribes inhabiting the Iraq were scarcely more obedient to Ottoman command than those who roamed the vast Arabian steppes— men who have the tradition of a personal independence which was limited only by their own customs, entirely ignorant of a world which lay outside their swamps and pasturages, and as entirely indifferent to its interests and to the opportunities it offers, will not in a day fall into step with European ambitions, nor welcome European methods. Nor can they be hastened. Whether that which we have to teach them will add to the sum of their happiness, or whether the learning of inevitable lessons will bring the proverbial attribute of wisdom, the schooling must, if it is to be valuable, be long and slow. In our own history from the Moot Court through Magna Carta to the Imperial Parliament was the work of centuries, yet the first contained the germ of all that came after. The tribes of the Iraq have advanced but little beyond the Moot Court, and should the shaping of their destinies became our care in the future, we shall be wise to eschew any experiments tending to rush them into highly specialized institutions—a policy which could command itself only to those who are never wearied by words that signify nothing,

Mesopotamian Outposts of Civilization.

In the life of the Arabian deserts there is little to which the passage of time brings alteration. The inelasticity of physical conditions confines the enterprise of mankind to limits which are exceedingly narrow. The sparse rainfall, the meagre supply of underground water, prohibit any extensive agricultural development. On the wide central steppes of the peninsula and the arid northern sands, the human race can find no abiding place, and the nomads pasturing their camels roam at the bidding of the herds over country where even the scantiest needs of man and beast cannot be furnished permanently. From time immemorial the inland tribes have supplied their wants from the nearest watered and cultivated land, where a sedentary population can raise in its rich fields and palm groves what is lacking to the hungry children of the wilderness, where crafts flourish and a man may find woven stuffs for his raiment and metals fashioned into weapons and household gear. Just as Joseph's brethren came down into Egypt to buy corn when a season of exceptional famine drove them beyond their

customary markets, so the wandering Arabs of
to-day come down out of the perpetual famine
of the desert into the borders of Syria and Mesopotamia for their elementary requirements.

The eastern towns of Syria, Damascus, Homs,
Hamah and Aleppo, are all markets for the Badawin
of the Syrian Desert, indeed Damascus is now, as
she has been in the past, at once the metropolis
of the wilderness and of the settled country, the
very centre of Arab civilization in all its aspects.
On the eastern side of the Syrian Desert the towns
of the Euphrates play a similar part. None of
those along the lower reaches of the river date
from a period earlier than the Mohammedan
invasion, though the modern Najaf is the representative of Kufah, one of the earliest camp-
cities of Islam, and Kufah itself rose out of the
ruins of Hirah, the capital of a small Arabian
principality which, before the time of the Prophet,
served as a link between nomad Arabia and the
empire which the Sasanian Kings ruled from
Ctesiphon. Just such links are to be found
to-day, south and west of the Euphrates—settlements which partake more of the nature of an
oasis in the heart of the peninsula than of a constituent of the cultivated regions of which they are

the outposts, tribal towns, as essential to the economics of Arabia as was Hirah itself, and in all probability not very dissimilar, except in degree, from that ancient seat of independent princes.

It is an advantage when the Badawin market-places lie beyond the limits of continuous cultivation, or at any rate upon its outer margin. The wild caravan drivers from the interior are apt to disregard the rights of the fellahin and to allow their beasts to pasture in crops carefully tended and irrigated, a negligence which results in reprisals on the part of the husbandman and a regrettable disturbance of public peace and security. On the other hand the incomers are not anxious to penetrate into the bilad al mahkumah, the governed lands, or to find themselves cooped up in cities and forced to submit to the restrictions which town life imposes. "A month in Damascus is like a year in the tents" observed a border chief who had been detained by the authorities till non-remitted sheep-taxes were forthcoming. "Wallahi ! I could not breathe there."

The Ottoman Government recognised the merits of placing the markets somewhat remote from the centres of civilization and favoured the foundation of outlying towns. Incidentally they extended thereby their own sphere of influence, since they exercised some control over the new settlements. A number of these might have been strung out along the edges of the desert if the Turks had been able to give sufficient protection to the community in its early struggles with robber and raider. An instructive example, though it proved a failure, was the attempt made a few years ago by a Shaikh of Jof in northern Arabia to establish himself permanently in the great ruined castle of Ukhaidhir, which lies some 8 hours to the west of Karbala. There were springs of water in the adjacent valley, while gypsum beds and good stone quarries were near at hand ; he was weary, said the Shaikh, of the government of Ibn Rashid, his overlord at Jof, and if the Wali of Baghdad could help him, he would build a town round the castle, plant palm groves and set up as a barterer of Mesopotamian produce against camels, an industry which might be of no small service to official transport departments. But the Wali had more pressing business, or perhaps his arm was not long enough to enforce order 8 miles from Karbala ; and in the end the Jof Shaikh was harried out by the local tribes who were accustomed to enjoy the water and grazing in the Wadi

Ubaid and looked jealously upon the intruder. He returned with his people to Jof, a poorer man than when he set out.

In just such manner, only with a happier ending to the history, sprang up in recent years the little township of Khamisiyah, at present in our hands. It lies to the south of the Euphrates, a few hours from Suq al Shuyukh, the older Market of the Shaikhs which is now neglected by their caravans in favour of the more accessible Khamisiyah. It owed its inception to a Shaikh of the Qasim province of Najd, in Central Arabia, Abdullah all Khamis, who called the town after his father. Its first years were precarious enough. Abdullah and his followers, all Sunnis from Najd, built themselves a tiny fort in which they held out against the nightly sniping of the surrounding tribes, who saw in the efforts of the Najdis to establish this small haven of security and industry, a menace to their position in the unruled desert. Gradually the place grew, more men came up from Najd, built their houses round Abdullah's fort and accepted his overlordship. From the Euphrates, also, some of the Shiah tribesmen came down to Khamisiyah and, abandoning their own Shaikhs, attached themselves to Abdullah's group. The Ottoman Government established a military post there, and the little settlement was strong enough to protect itself against all comers and to refuse or permit musabilah, access, to Badawin caravans.

More important, and of far more ancient origin is Zubair South-east of Khamisiyah and West of Basrah, to both of which places we shall shortly link it by rail. Zubair, which is old Basrah, goes back to the earliest days of the Mohammedan conquest. Like Cairo and Kufah it was one of the camp-cities which the conquering hordes laid out to suit the first needs of the occupation—Misr they were called, and the title has survived in Egypt where the whole land is named in Arabic Misr or Masr until this day. Like all Misrs, Zubair had its open space, bounded first by ditches and then by columned galleries, to serve as mosque of assembly, the common meeting place for weekly prayer and exhortation to which the believers in the new creed were summoned each Friday at mid-day. A fragment of brick minaret and wall still remain among the ruin heaps to show that the great mosque stood not far from the former channel of the Euphrates, for, as the Khalif Umar al Khattab had directed, the Misr was placed

within easy distance of water on the one hand, and
desert pasturage on the other. But when the
river changed its course Basrah changed its position ; it moved east, leaving nothing on the old
site but a little desert town, now called Zubair
after a famous warrior of Islam whose tomb it
contains.

With the defection of the Euphrates, it became
no more than a rather poorly supplied oasis
standing among extensive ruin mounds, but it is
clean and fresh like all towns in the dry clean air
of the desert. Sweet well water is lacking and
must be brought from outside, and nowhere in the
territories of Zubair is there more cultivation
than a few cornfields and some gardens of justly
renowned melons. The melon patches round
Barjisiyah and the cornfields of Sha'aibah are
now seamed with British and Ottoman trenches,
and a tamarish wood at Sha'aibah shelters the
graves of British soldiers who fell in the battle
of April, 1915. Here a new chapter in the long
history of Zubair was begun.

Men of Najd founded the town and they are
still almost its only inhabitants. The merchants
of Central Arabia come up and settle here, or some
member of a family of traders opens a branch in

correspondence with his relatives in Qasim or
Sudair. One of the best known of the Central
Arabian commercial families has representatives
at Jiddah, Damascus, Khamisiyah and Zubair,
and not a tribesman but is familiar with the name
of Bassam. The forebears of the present ruling
Shaikh came from Huraimlah in Sudair and were
subjects of Ibn Sa'ud, ruler of Najd. Like him
they belong to the powerful Anazah tribe. Besides
the town dwellers, there are a couple of hundred
tents of nomads, fractions of neighbouring tribes
who have attached themselves to the Zubair
community and own allegiance to its Shaikh. In
summer they draw in near the wells, sheltering
themselves from the fierce heat under admirable
huts of reed matting, one of the contributions to
architecture of tribal Mesopotamia ; but when
the rains have fallen they drive their sheep and
camels, together with those of the citizens of
Zubair, into the new-springing desert grazing
grounds. The method of their admittance under
the ægis of the Shaikh is as simple as that of
the Arabian oasis families. They ask and receive
permission to use his pastures and camp on his
land, and after they have sojourned his
territories for some time they are recognised a

belonging to him and not to the ruling houses of
their own tribe. He becomes responsible to other
tribes and to the Government for their good
behaviour, and if an enemy falls upon them and
loots them, it is he who will enter into negotiations
for the restitution of their property, even if the
hostile tribe should happen to be the very one to
which they formerly belonged. This process of
re-grouping, singularly well illustrated in a place
like Zubair, is not confined to border towns or
oases. Whole tribes have been formed in a
similar manner, some recently, some at the very
remote periods ; but recent or remote, the fact
that they are an agglomeration of units from
different tribal confederations is not forgotten—
in Badawin language they have no common ances-
tor. Homogeneous tribes will, however, readily
admit a stranger group, who in course of time will
lose all touch with their own people, though they
usually maintain slight differences of custom
which distinguish them from the people of their
adoption. Thus the amalgamation of divergent
elements under a common Shaikh falls well
within tribal custom.

Unlike Khamisiyah, the Mesopotamian tribes
are almost entirely absent from Zubair, or re-

presented only by a few donkey drivers who ply
between Zubair and Basrah. And being Najdi,
Zubair is also wholly Sunni. The people marry
among themselves, or take brides from the inner
oases, preserving the high bred type, the fine lean
physique, and the quick intelligence of the Badu.
And Badu even the Turkish Government,
usually unsympathetic in such matters, recognised
them to be, leaving them to a practical independence under their own Shaikh and not attempting
to impose upon them military service, from which
all Badawin were exempt. If they suffered little
from Ottoman interference, they benefited little
from official protection. The ruling Shaikh con-
ducted his own foreign policy with the desert,
and provided, by diplomatic means if possible,
security for his people. He was strong in the
position that the tribes would not willingly quarrel
with the owners of market towns to which they
were accustomed to resort.

But if they serve the Badawin, these frontier
posts of civilization are no less significant to the
administrator of the settled lands. They are
eyes and ears through which he can see and hear
what passes beyond his borders. From the
nature of his position it is essential that their

Shaikh should be in the closest touch with the
politics of the wilderness, and his sources of
information are innumerable. Every caravan
from the interior brings him news from the re-
motest parts of Arabia, every wandering tinker
and farrier who comes in to sell his load of firewood
and buy with the proceeds a pouchful of tobacco
and a handful of dates, gives him the local gossip,
where so-and-so is camped, whither such another
has gone, whose authority is on the wane and
whose is increasing, what disturbances are brewing
and what fresh combinations have taken place.
The Shaikh's coffee gathering hums with gossip
which, if he is experienced in such matters, he can
gauge and elucidate, and impart, if he is so disposed, to the nearest provincial governor. The
latter will find himself provided, not only with the
best and latest information concerning his frontiers,
but also with an intermediary whose intimate
relations with the independent tribes enable him
to perform many a delicate piece of negotiation
which would be beyond the power, or beneath
the dignity, of high official personages, and so
contribute to the maintenance of a good understanding and of peace along marches impossible
to fortify and difficult to guard.

The
Independent Chiefs of Eastern Arabia.

THE settled lands watered by the two great
rivers of Mesopotamia are bordered to the south
and west by deserts which are the home of nomad
tribes. The line of demarcation between the
Badawin and the Fellah n is not, however, an
ethnological frontier, nor is it a sharply defined
economic or political boundary. The cultivator
of rice fields and palm gardens is of the same race
as the wanderer in the desert ; in the past, and
often in a past not very remote, his forebears
dwelt in the black tents ; his habits of life have
undergone little radical change, and his ways of
thought have suffered no alteration. After the
winter rains half the village will revert to a nomadic
existence ; with their tents and household goods
borne on donkeys, they will drive their flocks out
into distant grazing grounds, where they will
remain until the grass has withered and the water
pools are exhausted. Hospitality in turn is
extended by them to their neighbours in the
wilderness, who in the height of summer come in
to the permanent waters and to the comparative
sufficiency of pasturage near the rivers.

But the dependence of the desert upon the
cultivated lands implies much more than a summer
visitation from the outlying tribes. The desert
does not produce so much as the necessities of
existence ; not even the oases of Central Arabia
are self-supporting, and nowhere are there any
industries for the manufacture of the elementary
utensils which the Badawin require, the clothes
they wear, or the arms with which they defend
themselves from their enemies. For all these
essentials they must come to the inland towns
and to the seaports, and they must, therefore,
remain on good terms with the people who
inhabit them and with the Government which
can forbid them access to the markets. Thus it is
that not only can remote parts of Arabia be controlled from without, but the rulers of the settled
countries must inevitably find themselves thrown
into economic and political relations with the
independent shaikhs whose wants they only can
supply.

Before the occupation of Basrah, the British
Government had already come into contact with
the Chiefs of Eastern Arabia, but except for a
treaty with Ibn Sa'ud in 1866 we had confined
our dealings strictly to those whose territories

bordered the sea. With the Sultan of Muscat, the Shaikhs of the Trucial Coast, and the Shaikhs of Bahrain and Kuwait we had long had agreements, some of which dated back as early as 1820, our main objects in every case being the preservation of commercial security in the Gulf and the suppression of traffic in slaves and in arms. Our interests were brought more sharply into line with those of the Shaikh of Kuwait, at the northern end of the Persian Gulf when, in 1899, certain foreign Powers seemed to be turning their attention to Kuwait as a possible terminus of a Mediterranean-Baghdad line. The Shaikh saw in that suggestion a fatal end to the position of virtual independence which he had succeeded in maintaining; the British Government saw in it the ominous beginning of a Teutonised Turkish supremacy over waters which, for more than a century, we had policed and lighted, and where our trade was still of greater value than that of any other country. We cut short years of dalliance with Ottoman susceptibilities, during which the Shaikh had never felt certain whether at the last resort we would or would not support him in his efforts to checkmate the pretensions of Constantinople, threw our influence into his scale, and extended to him such protection as the nominal subject of another Power could enjoy.

A year and-a-half before the outbreak of war with Turkey, another potentate, who for years past had been seeking for an opportunity for closer relations with Great Britain, forced himself into our line of political vision. Ibn Sa'ud, ruler of Najd, that is to say, of the oases and desert of Eastern Arabia, overran the province of Hasa, which had formerly been in the possession of his house, and pushed down to the shores of the Gulf, ejecting the three small garrisons which upheld the rule of the Sultan. Abdul Aziz Ibn Sa'ud, perhaps the most striking figure in recent Arabian history, has known every vicissitude of fortune, though he is not yet past middle age. He and his father were turned out of Riyadh, their capital, by their northern rival, the Amir of Jebel Shammar, M· hammad Ibn Rashid, who was the dominating personality of his day in Northern and Central Arabia. For several years Ibn Sa'ud wandered in exile, seeking refuge for a time in the Syrian desert, in the tents of the great Anazah tribe, with whom he claimed kinship, while his father found hospitality with the Shaikh of Kuwait. But when, in 1897, Muhammad al

Rashid died, leaving no man of his own remarkable
quality to succeed him, Abdul Aziz was not slow
to seize an opportunity. Aided by the Shaikh
of Kuwait, he rode into Riyadh with a small
picked band of followers, and, by a master stroke
of daring, recovered the town. The tale of his
entry at the dead of night, of the swift overthrow
of Ibn Rashid's vice-regent, and of the subsequent
years of contest with the Shammar, which ended
in the re-establishment of his supremacy over
Central Arabia, has already grown into an epic on
the lips of Badawin storytellers and songmakers,
and when this hero of many battles swept over
the Hasa the Ottoman Government was not a
little perturbed. The Turks had lavished gifts
on Muhammad Ibn Rashid and his successors
and studiously cultivated their friendship, hoping
through them to maintain some measure of
influence in Central Arabia. Ibn Sa'ud's success
was not only a direct hit at their claims to sovereignty, but also the extension of his authority to
the Gulf presented the signal danger of opening
the deserts to the dreaded influence of that
watcher of coasts, Great Britain.

Whether we should have been able to preserve
our policy of non-interference with Central Arabian

affairs, or whether the proximity of Ibn Sa'ud to the sea would ultimately have drawn us, as the Turks feared and as he wished, into direct relations with him need not now be determined. The outbreak of war brought our consideration for the Turks to an end, and as soon as he was assured of our friendship Ibn Sa'ud cast away all shadow of allegiance to the Sultan.

The occupation of Basrah must inevitably bring us into touch with Ibn Rashid and the Shammar ; for though the building of the Medina Railway has made it possible to travel from Hail to Damascus in less than a week, the commercial intercourse of Ibn Rashid's oasis is all with the markets on the Euphrates. Every spring the Amir's caravans, 500 or 600 camels strong, make the fortnight's march from Hail to the Iraq to replenish the stores of corn and oil, tea, coffee and sugar which the unlimited hospitality of his palace demand, as well as to purchase the garments with which every tribesman who pays his respects to Ibn Rashid must be presented, in accordance with his rank and importance. By camel caravan the merchants of Najaf furnish their partners settled in Hail with the stock-in-trade of the bazaars. Of the markets frequented by the

Shammar two are already in our hands. The
little towns of Zubair and Khamisiyah, outposts
in the desert, depending respectively upon the
metropolitan Basrah and the provincial Suq al-
Shuyukh, the "market of Shaikhs" on the
Euphrates, are in the occupied territories. The
seaport of Kuwait is administered by our firm
ally. Ibn Rashid, therefore, unless he be willing
to keep the peace with us, will be reduced to seek
his supplies higher up the Euphrates, and even
there he is beginning to find access difficult. By
sea and land we hold the eastern neck of the
Arabian bottle.

The Shammar have suffered since the death of
Muhammad Ibn Rashid from inefficient and
imprudent leading and from family jealousies,
resulting in bloody upheavals in the ruling house.
The present Amir is a boy of eighteen, untrained
in statecraft, ungoverned in temper, and lacking
in wise advisers. He clings blindly to the old
policy, which has hitherto proved very profitable,
of close adherence to Turkey, and shows no lean-
ings towards the pan-Arab sentiment, with which
from time to time the Shaikh of Kuwait and the
ruler of Najd have coquetted—for reasons not
strictly connected with an Arabian patriotic

revival. Under the Amir's feeble rule the tribe is, as might be expected, divided against itself, but the Shammar are a proud and valiant people, possessors of their full share of desert virtues, and obedient to their old ideals of desert conduct. They must always be a factor in Arabian politics and a turn of the wheel might restore to them much of their former supremacy.

One other great tribal group touches the Euphrates. The Anazah, most powerful of all purely nomad confederations, roam the Syrian desert from the borders of Mesopotamia to the eastern frontiers of Syria. They wander north almost to Aleppo, and in those northern regions cross the Euphrates and occupy the rich pasturage of the Khabur. Over this wide area more than one shaikh bears sway. The tribe is divided into four main sections, of whom the Amarat come up to the confines of the Iraq. Their paramount chief, Fahad Beg Ibn Hadhdhal, is nominally the ultimate lord of all Anazah, though, in fact, his western neighbour, Ibn Sha'lan, who commands the Syrian side of the desert, is a more notable personage. Unlike the Amir of Jebel Shammar and the ruler of Najd, Fahad Beg has no fixed abiding place. He lives with his

tribe, true People of the Camel, who follow where
their grazing herds lead them. Yet the strong
castles of Ibn Sa'ud and Ibn Rashid are not more
impressive to the imagination than Fahad's
encampment. In spring you may find him in
the grassy steppes of the Syrian desert, with a
couple of hundred tents round him, widely scattered in complete security from attack, and
during many hours before you reach him you
ride through his camel herds, for the Anazah are
the greatest of all breeders. The old Shaikh
seated on fine carpets in his guest tent, with his
hawk and his greyhound behind him, offers a
picture of tribal dignity which the walled cities
and lofty halls of the Central Arabian Princes,
and their troops of armed slaves, cannot rival.

The Amarat scarcely come as far down south
as Samawah, on the Euphrates, their market
towns being Karbala and Najaf and smaller
settlements higher up the rivers. A certain
amount of Syrian merchandise—wearing apparel
and cotton goods—reaches them also through
the enterprise of Damascene traders, but for
provisions they are dependent on Northern Iraq,
and, therefore, on those who rule it. Fahad Beg
himself owns some valuable palm gardens which

are watered from the Euphrates, and whoever controls the river has some grip on the sources of his private fortune.

The Ottoman Government, save for its constant regard for Ibn Rashid's friendship—a relic of Abdul Hamid's statecraft—followed no consistent policy in its dealings with semi-independent shaikhs. The Pasha had no sympathy with nomad Arabs, and the half-educated townsman of Constantinople or Salonika, who misguided the fortunes of the State through the Committee of Union and Progress, looked upon them as abhorrent relics of barbarism. A strong Governor of the Iraq would chasten them, perhaps not wholly without reason ; but under his weaker successor their liberty ran yet more wildly into licence. Nazim Pasha might have held them, firmly, if not wisely, but the high positions of the Turkish hierarchy were precarious eminences, and after nine months of office at Baghdad the jealousy of the Committee brought about his overthrow. Yet the task of controlling the tribes of the desert should not be one of the most difficult problems of Mesopotamian adminis-tration. The diplomatic parleyings and the ala-rums of war which sound among the tents, the wildernesses which change hands, and the dynasties which topple down are of no concern to the rulers of the settled lands. It is enough for them that the *de facto* master of the wastes should show respect for frontier, road and rail, and for outlying cornfields. Rewards for the observance of agreements are easy to devise—they are familiar and time-honoured in all intercourse with tribal countries ; but for any breach the closing of the markets of Iraq and the Gulf is a swift and sure retribution.

A Ruler of the Desert.

THE visit to Basrah on November 27th of Ibn Sa'ud was an episode in the Mesopotamian campaign no less picturesque to the onlookers than it was significant to those who have studied the course of Arabian politics. For the past century the history of the interior of the peninsula has centred round the rivalry between the Amirs of Northern and Southern Najd, Ibn Rashid and Ibn Sa'ud. When 'Abdul 'Aziz, the present representative of the house of Sa'ud, was a boy of 15, the power of the Rashid touched its zenith ; the great Amir Muhammad, Doughty's grudging host, drove the Sa'ud into exile and occupied their capital, Riyadh. For 11 years 'Abdul 'Aziz eat the bread of adversity, but in 1902 the Shaikh of Kuwait, on the Persian Gulf, himself at enmity with the Rashid, saw in the young Amir a promising weapon and gave him his chance. With a force of some eighty camel riders supplied by Kuwait, 'Abdul "Aziz swooped down upon Riyadh, surprised Ibn Rashid's garrison, slew his representative and proclaimed his own accession from the recaptured city. The story of his bold adventure is part of the stock in

trade of Badawin reminiscence ; the arrival of the
tiny band at dusk in the palm gardens south of
the town, the halt till nightfall, the scaling of the
palace wall by 'Abdul 'Aziz and eight picked
followers, the flash of steel which roused and
silenced the sleeping foe, and at dawn the throwing
open of the city gates to the comrades of the
victor. The struggle was not over with the
capture of Riyadh. In a contest renewed year
after year 'Abdul 'Aziz recovered the territories
of his fathers and made for himself a name which
filled the echoing deserts. At length in 1913 his
restless energy brought him into fields of wider
political importance. He seized the Turkish
province of Hasa, formerly an appanage of Riyadh,
ejected the Ottoman garrisons and established
himself on the seaboard of the Persian Gulf.
He was already on terms of personal friendship
with Captain Shakespear, our Political Agent
at Kuwait, and nothing was more certain than
that his appearance on the coast must ultimately
bring him into direct contact with Great Britain ;
but before the difficult question of his precise relationship to Constantinople had been adjusted, the
outbreak of war with Turkey released us from
obligation to preserve a neutral attitude. In

the winter of 1914-15, Captain Shakespear made
his way for the second time into Najd and joined
Ibn Sa'ud who was marching north to repel the
attack of Ibn Rashid, engineered and backed by
the Turks. The two forces met towards the end
of January in an indecisive engagement in which
Captain Shakespear, though he was present as a
non-combatant, was wounded and killed. We
lost in him a gallant officer whose knowledge of
Central Arabia and rare skill in handling the
tribesmen marked him out for a useful and distinguished career. His deeds lived after him.
Less than a year later Ibn Sa'ud met Sir Percy
Cox, Chief Political Officer of the Occupied
Territories, and Chief Political Agent of the Gulf,
and concluded a formal agreement with Great
Britain. His close connection with us has received
public confirmation in a durbar of Arab Shaikhs
held at Kuwait on the November 20th, where
he was invested with the K.C.I.E. On that
memorable occasion three powerful Arab Chiefs,
he Shaikh of Muhammarah, who though a Persian
subject is of Arab stock, the Shaikh of Kuwait
and Ibn Sa'ud, Hakim of Najd, stood side by side
in amity concord and proclaimed their adherence
to the British cause. In a speech as spontaneous

as it was unexpected, Ibn Sa'ud pointed out that whereas the Ottoman Government had sought to dismember and weaken the Arab nation, British policy aimed at uniting and strengthening their leaders, and the Chief Political Officer as he listened to words which will be repeated and discussed round every camp fire, must have looked back on years of patient work in the Gulf and seen that they were good.

Ibn Sa'ud is now barely forty, though he looks some years older. He is a man of splendid physique, standing well over six feet, and carrying himself with the air of one accustomed to command. Though he is more massively built than the typical nomad Shaikh, he has the characteristics of the well bred Arab, the strongly marked aquiline profile, full-fleshed nostrils, prominent lips and long narrow chin, accentuated by a pointed beard. His hands are fine with slender fingers, a trait almost universal among the tribes of pure Arab blood, and in spite of his great height and breadth of shoulder he conveys the impression, common enough in the desert, of an indefinable lassitude, not individual but racial, the secular weariness of an ancient and self-contained people, which has made heavy drafts on its vital forces and borrowed little from beyond its own forbidding frontiers. His deliberate movements, his slow sweet smile and the contemplative glance of his heavy-lidded eyes, though they add to his dignity and charm, do not accord with the Western conception of a vigorous personality. Nevertheless report credits him with powers of physical endurance rare even in hard-bitten Arabia. Among men bred in the camel saddle he is said to have few rivals as a tireless rider. As a leader of irregular forces he is of proved daring, and he combined with his qualities as a soldier that grasp of statecraft which is yet more highly prized by the tribesmen. To be "a statesman" is perhaps their final word of commendation.

Politician, ruler and raider, Ibn Sa'ud illustrated a historic type. Such men as he are the exception in any community, but they are thrown up persistently by the Arab race in its own sphere, and in that sphere they meet its needs. They furnished the conquerors and military administrators of the Mohammedan invasion, who were successful just where Ibn Sa'ud, if he had lived in a more primitive age, might have succeeded, and failed, just as in a smaller field he may fail, in the task of creating out of a society essentially tribal a united and homogeneous state of a durable nature. Muhammad al Rashid was the classic example in the generation before our own—he has been dead twenty years, but his fame survives. Like him 'Abdul 'Aziz has drawn the loose mesh of tribal organization into a centralized administration and imposed on wondering confederacies an authority which, though fluctuating, is recognised as political factor. The Sa'ud have in the palm groves of Riyadh and the oasesof their northern and eastern provinces, Qasim and Hasa, wider resources, greater wealth and a larger settled population than the Rashid, and their dominion rests therefore on a more solid foundation ; but the ultimate source of power, here as in the whole course of Arab history, is the personality of the Commander. Through him, whether he be an 'Abbasid Khalif or an Amir of Najd, the political entity holds, and with his disappearance it breaks.

If the salient feature of the Kuwait darbar was the recognition by the assembled Arab Chiefs of the goodwill of Great Britain towards their race, it was the presence of an unchanging type of desert sovereignty, among conditions so modern that they had scarcely grown familiar to those

who created them, which gave Ibn Sa'ud's visit to
Basrah its distinctive colour. In the course of
few hours the latest machinery of offence was
paraded before him. He watched the firing
of high explosives at an improvised trench and
the bursting of anti-aircraft shells in the clear
heaven above. He travelled by a railway not
six months old and sped across the desert in a
motor car to the battlefield of Sha'aibah, where he
inspected British infantry and Indian cavalry, and
witnessed a battery of artillery come into action.
In one of the base hospitals, housed in a palace
of our good friend, the Shaikh of Muhammarah,
he was shown the bones of his own hand under
the Rontgen ray. He walked along the great
wharf on the Shatt-al-Arab, through the heaped
stores from which an army is clothed and fed,
and saw an aeroplane climb up the empty sky.
He looked at all these things with wonder, but
the interest which he displayed in the mechanism
of warfare was that of a man who seeks to learn,
not of one who stands confused, and uncon-
sciously he justified to the officers who were his
hosts the reputation he has gained in Arabia for
sound sense and distinguished bearing.

" It is good for us " and the Shaikh of Muham-

marah, as the two Chiefs took their leave, " to
see your might. " Those who heard him may
well have found their thoughts reverting to a
might greater and more constant than that of
the War Lord, and looked forward to the day
when we shall expound the science of peace
instead of the science of destruction.

The Pax Britannica in the Occupied Territories of Mesopotamia.

THE history of the Mesopotamian campaign has a double aspect. Side by side with the tale of conquest by arms runs the story of victories no less renowned, the peace of Great Britain invading in the track of her armies lands to which peace had long been a stranger. Before the smoke of conflict has lifted, within hearing of the guns, the work of reconstruction has been initiated, and in spite of restrictions which a state of war cannot fail to impose upon the civil population, if the Expeditionary Force, with its train of civil and administrative officers, were to be withdrawn to-morrow, it would leave behind it a memory of prosperity, of incipient order, security and well-being.

To carry on civil government in an occupied country is a task which presents special difficulties. The administrator is hampered by the proximity of hostile influences, by divided allegiance and by the uncertainty of his own position. The last is a serious factor among the Arab subjects of Turkey, who are well aware that any obedience they may yield to the powers that be would serve as an excuse for pitiless retribution if a turn in the fortunes of war should reinstate their former masters. The fall of Kut has already furnished a forbidding example of Ottoman vengeance. The Turkish official was of a different race from those whom he governed, and it is partly because the population of the Occupied Territories have merely passed from one alien ruler to another that the change has been effected with comparative ease ; on the other hand, he shared with the majority of his Arab subjects a common creed, and unsympathetic as he undoubtedly was towards Arab civilization, he was yet provided with that understanding of Asiatic for Asiatic, which in spite of the deficiencies of Oriental administration give it an advantage over more adequate European methods.

In the derelict provinces of Turkey, the new ruler inherits little more than a formula of Government and must begin by converting it into an efficient reality. From Kut al Amarah to the Persian Gulf, the Wilayet of Basrah presented in Turkish times a comprehensive picture of lawlessness. On the Tigris, it is true, an intermittent control had been maintained, largely by playing

upon the hereditary enmities of great tribal
groups and the personal rivalry which existed
between individual members of the ruling houses.
To recognize local domination and yoke it to his
service lay beyond the conception of the Turk,
and the best that can be said for his uneasy seat
upon the whirlwind was that he managed to retain
it. In the Euphrates valley it may frankly be
admitted that he had been dismounted. Yet
if ever the precept which connects empire with
disunion should have held good it was in the 2,000
or so of square miles on either side of the river
from Qurnah to Nasiriyah. Marsh, rice-swamp,
desert and palm grove are occupied by some fifty
distinct tribes, all of which had at one time formed
part of the Muntafik league under the powerful
Hijaz family of the Sa'dun, while most of them
are still in name constituents of that famous
confederation. Until recently the Sa'dun contented themselves with tribute, military service
and the honours of chieftainship, claims which
the tribal owners of the soil acknowledged with
varying readiness ; but the relations of landlord
to overlord did not fall within the four corners
of the Ottoman definition of proprietory rights,
and in 1871 Midhat Pasha, then Wali of Baghdad,

effected a settlement on Turkish lines. The tribal lands were partitioned between the Crown and the Sa'dun and registered in Turkish title-deeds; the tribes found themselves reduced to the status of tenants and the Sa'dun bartered their ancient tribal prerogative for the questionable satisfaction of official support in their new rôle of landlord. The tribes have never acquiesced in this change. Acute agrarian discontent has kept the Muntafik district in constant rebellion, attempts to suppress the insurgents ended very commonly in the discomfiture of Ottoman arms, and since the weakening of the Central Government, consequent on the Italian and Balkan wars, neither the Crown nor the Sa'dun have succeeded in collecting more than a fraction of their rents.

Here also the Turks pursued their classic policy of attempting to improve their own position by the destruction of native elements of order. In a country parcelled out between a multitude of small units, each one well provided with ancient feuds, material was ample. The bonds of union which existed were consistently weakened, any shaikh who showed capacity for exercising control was countered by official hostility and intrigue, group was pitted against group, tribe against

tribe, and section against section, until through
the chaos which ensued neither Turkish official
nor merchant, nor traveller could secure safe
passage. Each petty chieftain built himself a
mud tower from which he defied, not unsuccess-
fully, such part of the universe as came within
his ken, or sallied forth in his light mashhuf to
plunder by marsh and canal his neighbours and
the passing stranger.

Into this prevailing anarchy, enhanced if
possible by European war, the British administration entered with the occupation of Nasiriyah
and Suq al Shuyukh in July 1915. To north and
south, the Turks and their adherents were ready
to tempt the tribes with bribes and promises;
military needs imposed measures, such as the
blockade of goods passing to the enemy, which
were galling to the population, and apart from
circumstances connected with the war, the habit
of social order is a delicate plant to rear. Yet
the periodical reports of local political officers
bear witness to the wisdom of the measures adopted and to the results which they have achieved.
Influential headmen have received recognition
and have been made responsible for their communities. Arbitration on the basis of tribal

custom is encouraged ; petty disputes over boundaries are adjusted, and with the help of shaikh and saiyid, blood feuds are adjudicated and squabbles peacefully settled. Faithful dealing with individual disturbers of the peace is limited by the fear of rousing a hornet's nest which might embarrass military operations elsewhere, but on occasion a tower has been knocked down and a malefactor handed over to justice with no other force behind the civil arm than a band of tribal guards enrolled within the last twelve months. Schools and dispensaries are being instituted and are eagerly welcomed, and a beginning has been made in the collection of revenue.

On the Tigris, there was no fundamental agrarian grievance. Lands which had been annexed by the Crown were still leased in large estates to the original tribal owners, though at rents immoderately swollen by the habit of putting up the lease to auction every five years. The first task, therefore, was to determine what sum could reasonably be claimed from the farmer. All arrears were remitted and in some cases the rent was reduced by half, probably with little loss to the exchequer as the nominal obligation had never been fulfilled. Old-standing quarrels arising from

undefined boundaries have been given a temporary
settlement based on the best local opinion available, and full advantage has been taken, in the
preservation of the public peace, of the responsibility of the shaikh, a principle well understood
among the powerful riverain tribes.

That the political officers in all parts of the
Occupied Territories have been skilful in exercising
a happy combination of force, patience and
persuasion is shown by the personal friendship
and confidence which exists between them and
many of the shaikhs with whom they have to
deal. These sentiments were clothed in ingenu
ous words by a chieftain from a wild Euphrates
swamp who had himself been a thorn in the flesh
of Ottoman officials. His comment on the
activities of the assistant political officer with
whom he had come into contact was prompted
by a profound acquaintance with his own country
side. "There are among the Arabs," he observed,
"a great number of liars and scoundrels, but
he knows how to distinguish good from evil."
A similar appreciation of the civil administrator
of his district, formulated by one of the best of
the paramount shaikhs of the Tigris bore no less
genuine an impress. "Never do I go to his

house," said the shaikh, " but he gives me a fair welcome." And encouraged by the treatment which had everywhere been meted out to him, he brought down his sick brother, a man who had spent his life in active conflict with the Turks, to die, as it proved, in the arms of the British Government at Basrah.

Not least among the elements of persuasion are the constructive works which have been undertaken, mainly for military purposes, along both rivers. Railway, road and dyke have proved that the word Government has a new significance and already a comparison is drawn between the constructive energy of the British and the devastation which marked Ottoman rule. " The gradual progress of the railway," says a recent report from a district on the Euphrates," is having a wonderfully calming effect. Perhaps more than anything else the advent of the line has quieted the tribes. The change from their almost openly hostile attitude last March has been remarkable. The permits issued to Arabs to travel by rail to Basrah did good. Many townsmen and tribesmen have ridden out to railhead on a visit of inspection, and all came back impressed." The impediments to commerce created by war, the lack of river transport, the shortage in imported wares, the blockade, and the enhanced price of living due to the exceptional demands of a large army, are compensated by the abundant and well remunerated employment which can be obtained both in the towns and in the country districts. On the whole the shaikhs have played up well in providing the labour demanded of them. Where the work, whether it were road or dyke, has been of benefit to cultivated areas it has proved a valuable political measure ; in one case the tribesmen themselves undertook the necessary repairs of an embankment.

The protection of the rivers and of the railway along the Tigris devolves upon tribal guards under civil control. Except for a few scattered posts, military protection along the main lines of communication as far north as Amarah is confined to the Nasiriyah railway through the desert, and even here tribal responsibility is not absent, for the friendly Badawin upon our frontier are charged with the maintenance of security in return for the subsidy they receive. On the Euphrates a small body of tribal horse has been enrolled to perform the duties of a civil police. The river guards had their prototype under the

Ottoman *régime* and the tribal horse correspond very closely with the Turkish gendarmerie ; service in either body has therefore a familiar air and is readily accepted. It is an outlet for restless spirits and, especially in the case of the mounted guards, it provides opportunity of honourable employment to petty chiefs and impoverished members of ruling families, such as the Sa'dun, whose loyalty to the British administration is proportionately larger according to their personal participation in local authority. Even if the number of these ·guards is as yet inconsiderable, they may be taken as one of many signs that the foundations of administration are being well and truly laid.

In exacting responsibility it is impossible to avoid a corresponding acceptance of responsibility. Whatever may be the issue of the war, the fate of those who have given us obedience and service in the Occupied Territories is a trust imposed upon national honour. Whether any plea of compulsion could avail with the Turk or the Teuton may well be considered doubtful. In many cases the obedience has been proffered too readily and the service performed too loyally to lend weight to excuses ; they would unquestionably meet with derision. Military occupation offers one of two courses, the policy of the iron heel or the policy of the administrator. The one is a blank negation of human endeavour, the other builds up a living organism which like all things living must fructify or perish. We have chosen the latter alternative and are charged with its fruit ; let the Belgian, the Pole and the Serbian bear testimony to the choice of others.

The
Shiahs and their position in the Iraq.

THE simultaneous announcement of the revolt
of the Hijaz and of the disturbances in Najaf
and Karbala, must fall upon the ears of the Mohammedan world with unparalleled significance. The
Ottoman Government has done its utmost to give
to the contest, into which, at the bidding of
Germany, it plunged Turkey and Arabia in the
autumn of 1914, the character of a Holy War
against the infidel. The Jihad was preached in
the mosques of Syria and Mesopotamia, and
during the whole course of the campaign in the
latter province, emissaries have circulated con-
tinuously amongst the Shiah tribes, urging them
to do battle in the name of the Faith. In Mesopotamia, indeed, some success was obtained; it
was not, perhaps, surprising that in Syria the
effects should have been *nil*, when it is remembered
that one of the preachers in the venerated mosque
of the Umayyads in Damascus was a German
Jew, too well-known in Turkish Arabia to be
accepted, even by the most ignorant, as an
authority on Mohammedan doctrine.

But the Ottoman failure to rouse Islam is shown by positive, not only by negative, manifestations. After a little over a year and-a-half of war, Arab independence of the Turk has been proclaimed from Mecca, the centre of the Faith, and the Persians of Karbala have sent a memorial to their co-religionists in Persia protesting against the outrages committed by the Ottoman soldiery on a Holy City and a sacred shrine.

In the Iraq, that is to say, from the head of the Persian Gulf up to Baghdad, the bulk of the population belongs to the Shiah persuasion, the proportion of Sunnis being comparatively small. The origin of the greatest schism of Islam goes back to the earliest days of the Faith, and is rooted yet deeper in the tribal divisions and jealousies which have ever proved the most serious bar to the political ascendancy of the Arab race. During his lifetime, the Prophet had laid down no definite injunctions as to the choice of a successor. His sons had died in infancy, his favourite daughter, Fatimah, was married to his cousin and adopted son Ali Ibn Abi Talib, whom he had pronounced openly to be more closely united to him than any other, but the democratic nature of the Prophet's teaching

would not seem to admit of the transference of his
office by direct descent, and in his own lifetime,
during a short illness, it was not his son-in-law Ali,
but his father-in-law Abu Bakr, whom he appointed to lead the prayers. The removal of
Mahammad's dominant personality was a critical
moment in the history of the new religion. The
Hashimid family, to which Ali belonged, insisted
that the position of Commander of the Faithful
and Viceregent of God devolved by appointment
as well as by succession upon Ali, but the choice
of most of the Quraish, the tribe of the Prophet,
and of some of the Companions, citizens of Medina,
fell upon Abu Bakr, and in this selection Ali
acquiesced. On the death of Abu Bakr he was
again passed over in favour of Umar Ibn Khattab,
another father-in-law of Mahammad, and when
Umar was assassinated in 644, the board of six
appointed by him to nominate his successor
elected Uthman Ibn Uffan who, with Ali, was
one of the six electors. It was only after Uthman
was murdered in 656 that Ali was raised to the
Khalifate.

H.s enjoyment of the dignity was broken by
two revolts. In the battle of the Camel near
Basrah, and in the battle of Siffin near Raqqah

on the Euphrates, he was called upon to uphold
his authority, first against Talhah and Zubair,
who fell and were buried at old Basrah (its modern
name, Zubair, is derived from the leader in the
struggle), and next against Muawiyah Ibn
Umayyah, the Governor of Damascus. The
fight at Siffin was inconclusive, for although Ali
remained in possession of the Iraq, Muawiyah
obtained the nominal Khalifate. He was not
recognised by the partisans of Ali, and after the
murder of the latter at Kufah, near Najaf, his son,
Hasan, was chosen Khalif by the Fatimids, the
adherents of the children of the Prophet's daughter
and Ali's wife, Fatimah. But Hasan refused
the honour and the house of Umayyah remained
in undisputed possession until the death of Muawiyah in 680. He had caused his son Yazid to be
acknowledged his successor, but Yazid met with
unexpected opposition. The people of the Iraq,
always hostile to the Syrian Umayyas invited
Husain, the second son of Ali, to claim the Khalifate, and Husain, trusting in the promises of the
unstable Iraqis, set out from Mecca with a party
consisting mainly of women and children. The
revolt was insufficiently prepared. When Husain
drew near to the Euphrates and camped on the

spot on which the town of Karbala stands to-day, he found that Yazid had the insurgents well in hand and within a day or two a body of 4,000 troops had cut off his camp from the river.

The story of the tragic events which filled the first ten days of the month of Muharram is recited in annual commemoration in every community of Shiahs and arouses a passion of anger and sorrow which the passage of over 1,200 years has been powerless to assuage. A Sunni Arab of Syria, recently escaped to Basrah from Turkish tyranny at Damascus, found himself during the course of his journey the guest of a Shiah tribe near Karbala. Sitting in the coffee tent at nightfall the Shaikh related to him the tale of Husain Ibn Ali—his faithful band, undaunted by the arrows of the enemy and the tortures of thirst, falling round him one by one, his son struck dead in his arms, his own lips pierced by a dart whilst he attempted to drink a cup of water, and as the recital proceeded, tears flowed down the cheeks of the Shaikh, and the tribesmen sitting round the hearth rocked themselves to and fro in an agony of weeping—" As if it had happened yesterday " said the astonished observer.

One sickly child, a son of Husain by a Persian

mother, escaped the general slaughter, and to him
and his descendants the Shiahs look as the true
Imams, heirs to the apostolical succession and
spiritual chiefs of Islam. Of these they recognise
12 since Muhammad, namely, Ali, his two sons,
Hasan and Husain, and nine direct descendants
of Husain, the last of whom, Muhammad al
Mahdi, vanished in the year 878, into a cave at
Samarra, north of Baghdad, before he reached
the age of 12. He, it is believed, will reappear
in the fulness of time and establish the universal
Khalifate. The pilgrimage to Mecca and Medina
is incumbent upon Shiahs as upon all Moslems,
but scarcely less prized is the pilgrimage to the
tomb of Ali at Najaf and of Husain at Karbala,
and in the vicinity of those shrines, especially
that of Najaf, every devout Shiah desires to be
buried.

The ecclesiastical leaders of the Shiahs, ex-
pounders and administrators of ecclesiastical
law, which covers nearly all civil cases, are the
Mujtahids, and it is the Mujtahids of Najaf and
Karbala who are of predominating distinction
and influence. Their functions are not only
religious ; they exercise a very strong political
suasion and are a power which the Turks have

had occasion to regard with dislike and distrust.
It is of importance to note that two of the signa-
tures, attached to the memorial recently sent to
Persia, were those of the son and nephew of one of
the best known Mujtahids of Karbala. The
Indian Government has long had relations with
Mujtahids of both cities, through whom distribu-
tion to the poor of the Holy Places, from the fund
known as the Oudh Bequest, are made.

The home of Shiahism is Persia and it is not
improbable that Aryan metaphysical thought,
originating in Persia, may have had some part
in shaping its doctrines ; its birth-place was
the Iraq, a province always deeply tinged with
Persian influence. So strong has been the per-
suasive force of local conditions upon the people
of the country, that Arab tribal immigrants from
the heart of Sunni Arabia have adopted the tenets
of the land and almost without exception have
become Shiahs. The process is still going on.
The Shuraifat, a purely nomadic tribe of the
Muntafik confederation, are probably recent con-
verts ; the Suhaiyim, a constituent of the Bani
Humaid section of the Muntafik, are still partly
Sunni, though to a very small extent ; and there
are even examples of conversion in the Sunni

family of Sa'dun, Ashraf, akin to the Sharif of
Mecca, and therefore of the purest Sunni stock.

The Sunni element in the Iraq, though small,
enjoys a social and political importance incom-
mensurate with its size. It consists mainly of
great landowners, such as the Sa'dun and the
houses of the Naqibs of Baghdad and Basrah,
and of wealthy merchants inhabiting the towns
and holding estates along the rivers. With the
exception of the Sa'dun, the Sunnis of the Iraq are
mostly town-dwellers. Since the country has
been under the Sunni Government of the Turks,
Shiahism has had no political status, Shiah
religious bequests have not had legal recognition, nor has Shiah ecclesiastical law, which
differs from that of the Sunnis, been included in
the Ottoman Code. Partly, it may be, because
of the unquestioned nature of the Sunni ascendancy, there has been little jealousy or bitterness
between the two branches of Islam in the Iraq,
and whatever changes the future may bring, it
should be the first care of the rulers of the country
to preserve that fortunate condition.

The radical difference between the teaching
of Shiah and of Sunni is on the question of the
Khalifate. By the Shiah no living Khalif is

acknowledged ; he awaits the coming of the Mahdi
who disappeared from human vision in the ninth
century. In the eyes of the Sunnis the claim of
the Sultan of Turkey is based upon the renunciation of the Khalifate and Imamate in favour
of Selim I by the last Abbasid Khalif of Egypt,
but it is difficult to reconcile the Sultan's title
with the doctrine very generally held by Sunnis
that the Khalif must spring from the tribe of
Quraish, a doctrine the authority for which is
derived from the Hadith, the traditional sayings
of Muhammad. Though it is not necessarily
a precept of the Faith that the Khalif should
wield both spiritual and temporal power, the
combination has great practical convenience, and
the fact that the Sultan of Turkey, alone among
Mohammedan potentates, was able to stand for
Islam militant, was overwhelmingly in his favour.
But the custody of the Holy Places was another most
important asset, and the anxiety of the Turks to
maintain their hold on Mecca and Medina was never
more apparent than in the efforts made by Abdul
Hamid to hasten the construction of the Hijaz Railway from Damascus to Medina. It was only because
of the extreme reluctance of the Sharif that the
line was not carried on from Medina to Mecca.

To the Shiahs the transference of political authority in the Hijaz from the Sultan to the Sharif cannot fail to be of moment, since it must affect the conditions of pilgrimage, but the pronouncement of the Sharif has a wider purport. To all Arabs, whether in the Iraq or elsewhere, the fixed purpose of the ruling power in Turkey to break and crush the Arab nation in every part of the empire must have become manifest. The persecution of the leading Arab families in Mesopotamia and Syria, the dismissal of the Arab officials, the declared intention to put an end to the official use of the Arab language, all these are indications of a policy which is perilous alike to Arab Shiah and to Arab Sunni, and it is the recognition of this peril which has inspired the Sharif to proclaim the independence of his race. In the danger of political extinction to which he and his countrymen were exposed, he has been the mouthpiece of deeply-felt and long-cherished aspirations towards liberty, which emanate not from Shiah, nor from Sunni, nor even exclusively from Islam, but from the most enlightened thinkers among the Arab people, irrespective of province or of creed.

Muhammarah.

FROM the mud flats of Fao up to Khaiyain creek, 11 miles above the mouth of the Karun River, the Shatt-al-Arab forms the boundary between what was once Turkey and what is still Persia. The Province of Arabistan, a tract isolated by mountains, river and marsh from Turkey and from Persia, has always maintained a semi-independent position, free from any but sporadic interference from either Power; nevertheless it was for long a subject of dispute between Tehran and Constantinople, whether Southern Arabistan should or should not form a nominal part of the dominions of the Shah, or to what extent it should form part of them. Persian influence has usually been predominant, but the population is almost entirely Arab, drawn from the neighbouring province of the Iraq. Towards the end of the 16th or the beginning of the 17th Century, the Arab element was further strengthened by the immigration of the great tribe of the Cha'ab, who were originally subject to Ottoman rule. The Cha'ab, wanderers like all the inhabitants of Mesopotamia from the Arabian peninsula, are said to have come from the western

shores of the Gulf, to have settled on the Gharraf,
at that time probably the main channel of the
Tigris, and occupied the lands round the city of
Wasit, now a wilderness of ruined mounds. They
were ejected by the powerful Muntafik confederation and moved on to the delta of the Karun
where they meted out to the local population the
same treatment which they had received at the
hands of the Muntafik, and extended east from
the Karun to the Jarrahi. As between Turkish
and Persian domination, the Cha'ab had no preference—both were equally distasteful to them ;
but when they spread eastward they came into
provinces which were undoubtedly Persian, and
they found themselves obliged to yield tribute
to the Shah. In the second half of the 18th
Century they were granted the Hindiyan lands,
east of the Jarrahi, and this was their farthest
extension in that direction. Nominally subject
to Persia, they were virtually independent ; they
appear in the troubled annals of Lower Iraq now
as allies of Persia, now as allies of Turkey ; on
the Shatt-al-Arab they followed the profession
of pirates, came thereby into collision with the
East India Company and laid themselves open to
somewhat ineffectual reprisals ; but in spite of

vicissitudes of fortune they remained practically supreme within their own territories.

In the beginning of the 19th Century a local rival stepped on to the stage. The Muhaisin, a tribe subject to the Cha'ab, founded Muhammarah near the junction of the Karun and the Shatt-al-Arab, and under an able and exceptionally long-lived Shaikh evinced a determination to throw off the Cha'ab yoke. Shaikh Jabir ruled his clan from 1819 to 1881. The favour of the Persian Government being always a doubtful quantity, he acquired large estates in Turkish territory that he might have a place of refuge and a means of livelihood in case of need, aided the British Government in its efforts to suppress piracy on the river, and incurred the suspicion of his Persian suzerain, who regarded relations between Great Britain and Muhammarah with a doubtful eye and was inclined to listen to the rumour that the Shaikh intended to throw off his allegiance and transfer his principality to us. His son, Miz'al, who succeeded him, was less well disposed towards us, partly because he was a competitor with us in the trade of the Karun, but Miz'al's younger brother, Khaz'al, was frankly pro-British, and even before his accession to power had given us assurances that he would do his utmost to further British commercial interests. Shaikh Miz'al was a grasping and tyrannical ruler; his assassination in 1897, though not due solely to public discontent, was welcomed with acclamation by the tribes, and his brother Khaz'al became by tribal election Shaikh of the Muhaisin and, by direct appointment by the Shah, Persian Governor of Southern Arabistan. The Cha'ab Shaikhdom had broken up (it was finally extinguished in 1898) and the Muhaisin had inherited the Cha'ab possessions from the Karun to Hindiyan, but Shaikh Khaz'al's personal right to these territories was not definitely established till 1903, when he was given by firman a secure title to all Southern Arabistan, with the exception of the Jarrahi estates which were owned by Persian landlords. They run wedge-like between H.ndiyan and the Karun, and the Shaikh's doubtful control over them is a constant source of difficulty. From his father and brother he held great estates in Turkish territory, to which he himself added until he became the largest landowner in the Basrah district. H.s influence there was enhanced by the fact that a very consi-derable proportion of the riverain population under Turkish rule were either Muhaisin or Cha'ab and looked to him as their tribal chief. The position was anomalous and brought into conflict the claims of territorial sovereignty (claims which the Arab is little accustomed to consider) with those of ancient tribal usage. The Muhaisin and Cha'ab, though living within Ottoman dominions, holding, when the Ottoman authorities could induce them to take them out, certificates of Turkish nationality and liable to conscription for the Turkish Army, brought all their disputes to the Sheikh of Muhammarah instead of into the Ottoman Courts and recognised his supreme jurisdiction and his right to call upon them for military service. Many possessed wheat lands in the Ahwaz district and would migrate thither during the mid-winter months to cultivate crops which lay 100 miles or more from their Turkish date-gardens. This divided authority over the tribes of the Shatt-al-Arab is one of the problems which confront the administration of Lower Iraq, but it is not a problem which presents any serious difficulty as long as we can rely upon the amicable co-operation of the Sha kh.

To the North-west the extension of Shaikh Khaz'al's authority to the turbulent Bani Turuf

brought the Hawizah marshes and pastures under
his control. The development of the Karun trade
gave Muhammarah a steadily increasing importance as the port of Central Persia, and Shaikh
Khaz'al's strong personality and marked friendship with the British Government did not tend
to allay the distrust which was aroused alike in
Turkey and in Persia by his growing influence.
His position with regard to Persia resembled
that of his neighbour and life-long friend Mubarak
of Kuwait in respect of Turkey. Both Shaikhs
enjoyed an autonomy which they were keenly
anxious to preserve, both feared the jealousy and
encroachment of their overlord, while the geographical situation of the one on the mouth of
the Karun and of the other at the head of the
Persian Gulf made them factors in commercial
questions of international interest which were
quickened into fresh vitality by the projected
Baghdad railway. Mubarak, who was a statesman of exceptional skill and foresight, played
for and ultimately won the support of Great
Britain. Khaz'al, a man of perhaps less ability,
but guided or at least assisted by a singularly
astute adviser in his Agent and Wazir, Haji
Muhammad Ali, the Rais al Tujjar of Arabistan,

adhered consistently to the assurances he had given
us before his accession and received in return such
help as was compatible with the preservation
of the integrity of Persia. In 1909, when he was
presented with the K.C.I.E., the Persian Government was informed that we had special relations
with him and that we would uphold him in the
event of any encroachment upon his rights.
The opening up of the Persian Oil Fields, and the
establishment of the Anglo-Persian Oil Company's
factory at Abadan, in the Shaikh of Muhammarah's
territory, cemented our commercial connection
with him; the occupation of the Basrah Wilayet
has made him a neighbour with whom it is essential that we should maintain those relations of
friendship and confidence which were established
before the war. His interests, both as a landlord
and as a tribal Shaikh, are not his only claim
to influence in the Occupied Territories. As a
powerful and practically independent Arab Chief
he is respected by all the tribes of Iraq, and the
fact that he is a Shiah gives him additional weight
among them. In Turkish times rebel Shaikhs
of the great tribes along the Tigris sought and
found protection with him, and to-day the Shaikhs
and Saiyids of the river banks will vaunt their

intimacy with him and make a point of paying him an occasional visit. Since the outbreak of war he has used his personal authority unfailingly on our behalf and given us all assistance which is consonant with his position as subject of a neutral State. He placed at our disposal, for use as a Base Hospital, a large house which he owned on the Shatt-al-Arab above Basrah, and when in the spring of 1915 certain unruly elements under his jurisdiction, incited by the preaching of the Jihad by Turkish emissaries, rose in revolt and assisted the Turks to attack our troops at Ahwaz and cut the pipe line, his steadfast attitude and his unshaken belief in our ability to deal with the situation, combined with our success at Sha'aibah, did much to prevent further secession and to facilitate the rapid restitution of order as soon as the Turks were driven across the Karkhah by the operations of the 12th Division. The chaotic condition of Northern Arabistan adds to the difficulty of his administration, but he has spared no effort to keep the tribes in hand, and to that end has subordinated his personal interests to immediate political requirements. In return we have maintained him in complete ownership of his estates in the Occupied Territories :

all further adjustment of his rights in the district he has been content to leave until the final settlement at the end of the war.

It would be difficult to picture a greater contrast than that which exists between the two leading personalities of Mahammirah, Shaikh Khaz'al and Hiji Rais. Shaikh Khaz'al is a tall man, massively built, with strongly marked but coarsely moulded features of a distinctly Semitic type which vouches for his Arab descent. He wears the old Cha'ab headdress, a black folded turban with a pendent end, and affects a certain richness in dress which accords with and enhances his commanding appearance. The Rais al Tujjar is a pure blooded Persian, small and alert in figure, with a finely-cut face, worn sharp by age. The pair, standing side by side, the head of the one barely reaching to the shoulder of the other, represent the intellect and the physical vigour which have brought the State of Mahammirah safely through the narrows, notwithstanding the menace of the Persian Scylla and the Turkish Carybdis.

Shaikh Khaz'al is fully aware that the future will demand of his successors more than personal courage and inherited prestige, if they are to hold their place in the new order which is dawning on Mesopotamia. He has placed his sons in an American Mission School in Basrah, and he does not fail to impress upon them that without education even the descendents of autonomous Princes will be outstripped in the race. The potential wealth of his country may be dimly gauged by its ancient prosperity, when the Sasanian monarchs Shaikh Khaz'al's remote Persian predecessors, held the Emperor Valerian captive, dammed the rebellious rivers of Arabistan and erected great palaces, of which the ruins fired the imagination of Arabian geographers of the 10th Century. A lurking ambition to rival Sasanian fame has moved the Shaikh to adorn with stucco counterparts of Sasanian rock cut reliefs the walls of his own palace at Failiyah, below Muhammerah, where imperfectly executed genii present wreaths of victory to invertebrate warriors who wear the arms, the bulbous crown and floating scarves of the Chosroes.

Notwithstanding the native quickness and adaptability of the Arab, a task yet more difficult than the emulation of Sasanian exploits lies before the Shaikh and his successors, and our responsibility for those who have put their trust in British civilisation extends beyond the care for their political security into regions which call for the exercise of infinite patience, and of the wisdom bought by experience not only of success but also of failure.

A Tribe of the Tigris.

THE Tigris is a river of Arabia. The merchant may regard it as a trade route, and the soldier as a line of communications, the geographer may score h s map with names ancient and modern, but no other definition will satisfy the ethnologist or guide the administrator. The Tigris is a river of great tribal confederations, immigrants frôm the deserts of the Arabian peninsula. Names that ring through the heroic legends of Arabia— Bani Tamim, Bani Rabi'ah—are to be found among them, and historical record confirms their claim to such high ancestry. No structural alteration in the nature of their social organization differentiates them from the B dawin of to-day, but their long sojourn in the Iraq has been productive of outward changes. They have become cultivators, or they take toll from the cultivation of smaller tribes, some of whom may represent an earlier stratum of population, while some are sections detached from other large Mesopotamian units ; they have been affected by local religious influences and have turned from the Sunni tenets of the desert to the Shiah creed which centres in Najaf and Karbala ; physi-

cally they have profited by ampler conditions of
living, and the powerful, big-boned type common
among them contrasts with the hungry s'enderness
of the B. dawin. But if they have gained in worldly
prosperity they have lost in honour. Their
brothers of the wilderness will neither give their
daughters in marriage to the Iraq tribes nor take
wives from among them. They are Ma'dan, a
loose denomination which applies generically
to the social level below that of the speaker. To
the Badawin all the riverside people are alike
Ma'dan ; on the lips of the cultivators the description refers to the buffalo owners and fishermen
of the marsh ; etymologically it means no more
than the dwellers in the 'Adan, the plain, which
by a confusion of ideas has become in our tongue
a synonym of Paradise.

The canals from the Tigris and the marshes
into which they fall had been so seldom visited
by Europeans during Turkish times that the
tribes and their mode of life were almost unknown
to us. The names Albu Muhammad, Bani Lam
and Bani Rabi'ah represented little more than
an amphibious population of insubordinate habits,
who at intervals unpleasantly frequent fired at
river steamers, held up traffic and defied Turkish

efforts to keep them in check. One of the great groups of the lower Tigris came in 1915 completely under British control, and we are beginning to form some idea of its composition and character. As an independent entity the Albu Muhammad are not of ancient date. According to their own account they are an offshoot of the Zubaid, a numerous and widely disseminated people, one of whose seats is in northern Iraq. Trustworthy dates are not furnished by local historians, but for the last nine generations the Albu Muhammad have had a separate existence on the Tigris between Amarah and Ezra's Tomb, their headquarters being the little town of Qal'at Salih. They have long since severed the links with their Zubaid ancestors and the one group takes no interest in the fortunes of the other.

Religious observance, as is commonly the case among genuine tribesmen, would seem to sit lightly on the Albu Muhammad, but they regard with deference the Saiyids, the descendants of the Prophet, who live among them, turning to them for the adjudication of disputes and respecting their awards. The cry of Jihad, widely published by Saiyids from the holy cities, brought the tribes out against us at the beginning of the war, but what part was played by a profound Mohammedan sentiment, and what by a natural desire to take a hand in any movement which gave pleasurable anticipation of lawlessness and loot would be difficult to determine. The Shaikhs showed no pertinacious devotion to the Turks, with whom they had spent most of their lives in active conflict. They made submission as soon as we had established ourselves at Amarah, and for the last 18 months they have shown themselves reasonably loyal, willing enough to meet unusual demands for labour on road and railway, and to hold cordial intercourse with British officials.

The land which they occupy is Ottoman Crown property and is leased out in periods of five years to the highest bidder, but the prescriptive right of the tribe to its own districts has limited the choice of lessees, and in practice the Turkish Government was unable to grant Albu Muhammad farms to any but Shaikhs of the ruling house. They hold and cultivate the area of great canals on either side of the river below Amarah, and people the marshes at the tail of the water ways. Cultivators and Ma'dan alike live in reed huts which are almost as mobile as the black tents of the Badawin, and within their own limits they

are still nomadic. Any tendency to permanent
settlement was checked by the fear of being
liable to conscription, but ruling Shaikhs own
property in the local town, Amarah or Qal'at
Salih—just as a chief of the western Syrian desert
will have a house in Damascus—and those who
have leased the same estate from term to term
over a number of years have built themselves
brick houses at their customary places of resi-
dence. The Shaikh's jurisdiction in all tribal
matters is supreme ; in this as in other particulars
the social order of the desert is faithfully repro-
duced. The women move freely and unveiled
among the tribesmen, and though the lot of the
average woman is equally unenviable in the reed
village and in the black tent, in both cases she
may on occasion play an influential part. Two
notable ladies are to be found to-day among the
Albu Muhammad, sisters and divorced wives of
Shaikhs, who have declined to embark on fresh
matrimonial adventure and have returned to the
home of their respective brothers. They manage
the lands allotted to them with no less vigour
than they show in directing the affairs of the
family. One of these Mesopotamian upholders
of the rights of her sex (candour compels the

admission that she is a shrew) was entrusted
by us for a brief period with a Government estate
when her stepson, the Turkish lessee, proved
intractable, but this task proved to be somewhat
beyond her powers. The other was in the habit
of accompanying her brother the Shaikh in his
official visits to Baghdad, and interviews when
she repairs to his town house at Amarah, the
brokers and merchants with whom he transacts
dealings in grain. A merry, determined woman,
she enjoys a gossip with a political officer on tour
and thinks nothing of a long journey by river
and canal if a bride is to be conveyed to the house
of a shaikhly relative—or for that matter of
hustling the newly wedded bride away again,
if she is not satisfied with the reception accorded
her. " Our daughters are fair as birds and gold,"
said she in describing a recent exploit of this
nature, and an expressive gesture left the imagination to conjecture the insufficiency of the
accommodation which had been provided for
such treasures. Nevertheless matrimonial rebuffs
must be rare, for the Albu Muhammad shaikhs
manage to contract an inordinate number of
marriages. From forty to fifty children is no
unusual family, and the household is increased

by a horde of domestic slaves whose negroid hair and features attest their African blood, though for the most part generations of Mesopotamian breeding have robbed them of their original complexion. Like the independent chiefs of Central Arabia, each ruling shaikh maintains an armed bodyguard, a hoshiyah, the members of which receive grants of land in return for military service.

What with his numerous family, his slaves and his hoshiyah, the shaikh's immediate dependents run into many hundreds ; in Arab fashion he keeps open house for all who come to pay him their respects ; his fees to Government amount on the richer estates to over £20,000 a year and were double that sum under the Turks, when rents were forced up by the periodical auctioning of the lease. But though he may not have much ready money at his command he is a rich man, living in abundance on the produce of his estate. His position depends on his power to give employment on the land and thereby keep his wandering cultivators together. The silting up of a canal will set the reed village packing, to the detriment of his tribal strength as well as his income. The possibility of large defections is a source of anxiety to him, for labour once scattered is with difficulty reassembled.

Physical conditions determine the composition of the Albu Muhammad community. Along the river and the main canals the ground is raised by silt deposits, with the result that the great water channels run through a low ridge instead of through a valley. On these ridges grow the winter crops of wheat and barley, an uncertain yield depending partly on the rainfall. Untilled tracts of scrub and thorn and small infrequent reed villages lend to the high ground a certain air of inhospitality. The cultivators are settlers drawn from weak neighbouring confederations, who take service under the wealthy Albu Muhammad Shaikhs and enter into tribal relations with their employers. As the ground falls towards the marsh the sparser husbandry gives way to continuous rice-fields, with an accompanying increase of population. The yellow reed huts, banked up in winter with rice straw to keep out the rain and the north wind, line the canals in long village streets. In spite of their frail materials they convey an impression of rural comfort and prosperity which is borne out by the appearance of their stalwart well-nourished inhabitants. These villages are the home of the Albu Muhammad tribesmen, who reserve the fertile rice country for their own use and profit, employing even here fellahin from the corn lands to execute for hire the heavier labours. The landscape ends in the reed and open water of the marsh, where the island hamlets of the Ma'dan occupy ancient knolls, rich in fragments of pottery, and the light pitch-covered mashhuf is the only means of communication.

Save for the brick-built house of the Shaikh, from river to marsh no permanent habitation is to be found among the cultivators, but just as on the edges of the desert small market towns have grown up to supply the needs of the Badawin, so on the canals there is an occasional settlement of townsfolk, clustered round a bazaar which is stocked with cotton goods, dates, coffee, tobacco and other simple requirements of the country side. Some shrewd merchant of Najd origin, easily distinguished by his finer features and superior education, presides over this group of shop-keepers and acts as Mudir on behalf of the Government. A Sunni, with a comprehensive contempt for his clients, from shaikh to marsh-man, he takes his wives from families of like

origin with himself, bringing them from Zubair
or elsewhere on the desert borders, and preserves
the Najd blood and the Najd tradition untainted
in the heart of Iraq.

Notwithstanding a prevailing turbulence under
Ottoman rule, the task of the administrator
would not seem to present overwhelming difficulties when once the tribal character of the Albu
Muhammad country is admitted and used to
advantage. The Turkish Government, too weak
to control the shaikhs, sought to undermine an
authority for which they could offer no substitute.
Instead of endeavouring to allay dissension, they
regarded intertribal and family jealousies as the
best guarantee against hostile combination, and
accepted local unrest as the less formidable of
two evils. Their methods, pursued with great
adroitness, were in so far successful that they
managed to maintain a semblance of administration which will prove a valuable heritage to
more capable rulers.

The Star Worshippers of Mesopotamia.

A CURIOUS phenomenon in Mesopotamia is the existence of a mass of people who have borrowed from all the races about them and have adopted customs belonging to all, and yet are totally isolated from them socially.

These are the Sabeans, known to some as the "Star Worshippers of Mesopotamia." Some writers have referred to them as "Saint John Christians," but this is a misnomer, because the "John" to whom they profess to adhere is certainly not a Saint, nor are they Christians in any sense of the word ; they are the Sabeans mentioned in the Book of Job, though not the Sabeans mentioned in the Quran. During the time of the Mohammedan supremacy, however, they have accepted the interpretation that they are the Sabeans mentioned in the Quran, in order thus to protect themselves against persecution, since the Sabeans are mentioned in the Quran along with Christians and Jews as "People of the Book" and, therefore, to be reverenced.

The scientifically correct name of these people is the Mandæans. The word Mandæan in their own language means "disciple" and they refer to themselves as the "Disciples of John." Their language is Mandaitic, which belongs to the Semitic group of languages, and is a first cousin of Syriac. No printed literature exists, although a few of their manuscripts are in the hands of European scholars. The foremost Mandaitic scholar was Peterman, a German Orientalist, who about 60 years ago spent two years among the Sabeans at Suq-al-Shuyukh. They, of course, also speak Arabic, though never to my knowledge have they attended any Arabic Schools.

In the 17th century they numbered about 20,000 families, but at the present day their total does not exceed 3,000 souls. They exist only in Mesopotamia, a few living in Baghdad, and by far the great majority around Suq-al-Shuyukh. They are never to be found at a distance from running water inasmuch as the tenets of their religion demand their proximity to living water. The great decrease in population is due first of all to the persecution from the Mohammedan and then to internal strife ; further many of their women have in late years been married to Mohammedans and thus the race is fast disappearing. They have three chief oc cupations, that of silver-smiths, canoe building and dairying. Their peculiar canoe is called the Mashhuf. Their silver work is justly famous for exquisite workmanship. It consists of black and silver wrought in cunning designs. The composition of this black substance, supposed to be antimony, is a secret of the trade with them. Of late years Arabs have been more tolerant towards them because of their ability as smiths and boat-builders, in neither of which occupations the Arab has any skill.

Their religion is a curious mixture of old Babylonian Paganism, of the Jewish Cult, of Christianity and Mohammedanism. From the Jewish religion they have borrowed sacrifices and purifications ; from the Christian religion they have borrowed the observance of the first day of the week, Baptism, the Lord's Supper and the reverence for John the Baptist and from the Mohammedan religion they have borrowed polygamy.

Their great book, called the Sidra Rabba, contains their doctrines in rather fragmentary form, and gives evidence of a variety of authors, and a great number of contradictions. Even a glimpse of this book is very difficult to obtain, although many efforts have been made to secure a copy. Some years ago some travellers succeeded in stealing a copy, but representations were made to the Consul and the book was returned to the owners. I understand that a copy exists in the British Museum, together with a poor Latin translation which has never been completed. In 1904, through the friendship of their Chief Priest, I was allowed to purchase a copy for the sum of twelve pounds (Turkish), but on the condition that I should never sell the same. Even then, the next day there was a great demonstration by all the Sabeans and earnest endeavours were made by them to compel me to return the book. The copy in question is now being translated in America. A curious feature of this book is that half of each page is reversed to allow of the book's being placed over a narrow channel of running water and read by a Priest sitting on either side.

Another of their books is the " Book of Souls," two-thirds of which consist of prayers for the living and one-third of prayers for the dead. This book also contains a history of the death of Adam, who to them is one of the greatest Prophets.

A third book contains Liturgy for the Priests, and others contain marriage ceremonial, the life of John the Baptist, a treatise on astrology and various formulas for incantation and sorcery.

Their belief is that the world originated from what is called a " First Fruit," something like the Orphean theory of the world egg, and that the Great Lord brought forth life from this great egg, from which life again emanated another life who was Jesus Christ, but that the latter endeavoured to usurp the power of the former, and was therefore placed among the Planets as Mercury. They believe that the Heavens consist of the purest water, so hard that not a diamond can cut it, in which flow all the heavenly bodies as well as this earth. They also believe that the earth is surrounded on three sides by seas, but on the fourth there is a turquoise mountain, the reflection from which gives the blue colour to the sky. They further believe that the Queen of Darkness married Fire, and brought forth 24 sons, of whom 7 were the Planets including the Sun, 12 were the signs of the Zodiac and the remaining 5 are not known. These Planets are sources of evil to mankind. The Pole Star is situated at the very dome of Heaven and therefore they pray toward it, and for this reason they are called the " Star worshippers."

They practice Baptism, which by the pious among them is received every Sunday ; they also observe a sort of Supper which apparently is an imitation of the Christian Communion.

They have places of Worship which, however, are only large enough to contain two or three Priests, and through these places of Worship run tiny streams of water over which prayers are said. There is no furniture in their Churches, save a shelf on which books and other articles are kept. Their priesthood is open to both men and women. The first grade is that of the novitiate, after which is the grade of Priest, thereafter a Bishop, and the highest official of the Church is the Chief Priest. The present Chief Priest is named Shaikh Mahi and resides at Suq-al-Shuyukh. No priest may have the slightest blemish in his body and the consequence is that the Chief Priest is one of the most striking figures I have ever seen anywhere. A woman may attain to the rank of priesthood, but only on the condition that she marry a priest. It is against their religion for them to wear dark clothes, and for their women to wear anything blue.

One wonders how this curious growth will fare in the new soil of British administration. They are unquestionably pro-British, for the reason that they have always been anti-Turkish.

They never cut their hair, and both men and women may be called decidedly handsome, in fact so handsome that a Sabean can be at once recognised.

They were taken into the Army by the Turks, but were again excused because of the utter impossibility of meeting their religious demand to be always near running water.

ASIATIC TURKEY

BY

GERTRUDE LOWTHIAN BELL.

CONTENTS

PREFACE.

These articles were written at the request of the War Office during June and July, 1917. It has been suggested that they might be of some interest to members of the Force serving in Mesopotamia who may not have had opportunity to make acquaintance with the Dominions of the Sultan beyond the battle-fields of Gallipoli and the 'Iraq.

G. L. B.

Office of the Civil Commissioner,

October 1917.

Asiatic Turkey.

A Survey.

In one of the seven Odes which are reckoned to be the masterpieces of ancient Arabian poetry, there is a description of the passage of a tempest across the face of the desert. The poet portrays, in verses famous for their rugged splendour, the gathering of the crowned clouds, the flash of the lightning, like the flicker of hands in the darkness, the rush of the mountain torrents driving the gazelles from their haunts, and the crash of palm trees and of dwellings in the oases. The hills, he says, were clad in the fury of the storm like a man wrapped in a great cloak. But when the devastation was over the drenched plains sprang to life with a patin of flowers "as though some merchant of the Yaman had spread out his many coloured wares" and the larks sang as if they had been intoxicated with aromatic wine; yet in the waterways lay the bodies of dead beasts "like bulbs uprooted from the earth."

To us, seated in Baghdad, the retreating menace of German domination over Asia appears in just such an aspect. For some of us the Mesopotamian campaign is but the last chapter in a history with which we have had a long familiarity. We watched the clouds crown the heavens, but alarming as the threat appeared, few foresaw the ferocity of the climax which was to devastate the West as well as the East; "from Dharib to Uthaib we saw it break" says Imrul Qais, as we might say "from Reims to Erzerum." Looking back over the revealed course of German ambition, her Asiatic dream appears as the index to that policy of merciless self-development which led to universal conflict, and it is scarcely too much to say that when the Emperor William placed his historic (and much derided) wreath upon the tomb of Saladin at Damascus, the train was laid which fired the artillery of the Somme. If the main battle had necessarily to be fought in Europe the reward was to be found chiefly in Asiatic Turkey, and there is a dramatic finality in the fact that the first salient victory of the war, the capture of the southern capital of Asiatic Turkey, should have been won in the very regions where Germany counted on remuneration for her gigantic efforts.

What then was the prize which was worth the life blood of so many thousands of Pomeranian grenadiers, and how was it to be won ? What is the actual condition of these lands where Germany intended to establish her eastern empire, and what is their promise ? There are few Englishmen who could support with any credit interrogation on the Asiatic Provinces of Turkey. To the tourist the absence of railways, combined with the extreme rarity of reasonably good roads and a corresponding lack of decent accommodation, were sufficient discouragements. A jaunt through the Holy Land, a glimpse of Smyrna and Ephesus and a few days at Constantinople were the high water marks of polite travel. If Damascus was reached the Orontes valley was beyond the pale and Aleppo a name. The interior of Asia Minor found no place in the suave pages of these Odysseys, and the Mesopotamian plains were innocent of dragoman-conducted tours. To the investor Turkish credit seemed too uncertain to repay detailed enquiry ; he could and did find better security for his capital elsewhere. It is true that, since the days of the Levant Company, Great Britain had been in commercial relations with Turkey, and old established houses in the coast towns of the Mediterranean continued the tradition, while British firms in Basrah and Baghdad still disposed of a greater volume of trade than could be claimed by any other nation. But from Smyrna and Baghdad alike business with the interior was carried on through native agents whose activities were circumscribed, like those of the tourist, by the absence of means of communication, to say nothing of the general uncertainty with respect to life and property which prevailed in the Ottoman Dominions. Comprehensive railway projects had been discussed and abandoned ; the British Government offered them no encouragement and showed a marked preference for abstaining from pledges which might lead, as pledges will, to entanglements. Thus the psychological moment had been allowed to pass, and not necessarily through a culpable indifference. British enterprise was embarked in other and safer channels ; Turkey was written off, with a vague regret that we had been so needlessly bellicose on her behalf as we had shown ourselves in the Crimean war, and a pious hope that we might under all circumstances be able to maintain our commercial position in Mesopotamia and a political ascendency in the Gulf which was regarded as vital to the safety of India.

It was in Germany that politicians woke the
public mind to a realisation of the potential wealth
which lay behind the façade of decay presented
by the Ottoman Empire and moved their fellow
country-men to an imaginative appreciation of
the advantages offered by eastern expansion.
But in German political philosophy a place in the
sun implies the exclusion of all others from enjoy-
ing the rays of that luminary, and the idea of a
Turkey which was to be the field for German
commerce speedily developed into the prospect
of a subservient Turkey, trained in arms under
German masters to be a weapon in the coming
struggle. A web of intrigue, disclosed to us
since the outbreak of war, was drawn across
Persia and into India for the overthrow of the
one European rival in Asia who was regarded
with real apprehension, but harmful to ourselves
as this propaganda may have been, it was to
Turkey that her German guides were to show
the way to ruin. The fatal ideal of militarism
strangled at birth the constitutional movement
of 1908. The money which should have been
spent in opening up and irrigating the country
found its way into the pockets of Krupp and in
unproductive expenditure on the Army ; and yet

more disastrous in an empire composed of many nationalities was the German policy of strengthening and supporting the Turk in his determination to trample under foot all other racial elements. Among Germans employed in Turkey, from military instructors to archæologists, it was an accepted principle that the Turk alone was worth backing. How far that principle could be carried has been illustrated during the war ; the massacre of the Armenians and the persecution of the Arabs were perpetrated in vindication of Ottoman sovereignty.

The Asiatic Empire of Turkey extends from the Black Sea on the north to the Persian Gulf on the south. It includes the whole of the mountain bridge between Europe and Asia which we know as Asia Minor, a country of lofty ranges and upland plateaux stretching west from the Persian frontier and dropping through fertile valleys to the coasts of the Black Sea and Mediterranean ; while enclosed between the Syrian and Kurdish prolongations of the Anatolian mountain systems, lie the vast pasture lands which are the southern basin of the two great Mesopotamian rivers. About the latitude of Baghdad, at a distance of some 350 miles from the Persian Gulf, the Euphrates and Tigris approach within 20 miles of one another, only to draw apart again and encircle an area of prodigious fertility, the province of 'Iraq. Nominally the Sultan's writ ran through Arabia, for practical purposes it went no further than the railway could carry it, namely, to the Hijaz ; and with the exception of this province and its two sacred cities, no other part of Arabia was of vital interest to Turkish rulers, though they poured out blood and money in the effort to maintain a precarious hold over the Yaman.

Roughly speaking, therefore, Asiatic Turkey fell into two parts, the mountains to the north and the plains to the south, the mountains being inhabited by Turks, Kurds and Armenians together with large colonies of Greeks—the latter mainly near the coast—while the plains are the dominion of the Arabs and can rightly be regarded as an extension of the Arabian peninsula. The western mountain border of the plains, that is to say the whole of Syria, has been from time immemorial the inheritance of immigrants from Arabia proper, while the eastern mountain frontier is in its northern and central parts Kurdish, while in its southern reaches it passes into Persia and is inhabited by tribes of Persian origin. With the exception of the Syrian ranges it is exactly in accordance with facts to assume that the hills mark the boundary of the Arabic speaking race. North-east of Baghdad, as soon as the ground begins to rise towards the low ridge of the Jabal Hamrin, the scene of recent fighting, the Arab population thins out and disappears, to be replaced by Kurdish tribes; and in the same manner at the northern limit of Mesopotamia where the immense plain lifts itself in long undulations towards the mountains of Anatolia, there again the Kurds people the villages and stream out in spring to mix with the Arab tribes in the desert pasturages. So constant is the avoidance by the Arabs of the high ground, that in the Jabal Sinjar, the ragged crest which cuts across the tribal areas of northern Mesopotamia about the latitude of Mosul, the inhabitants are almost wholly Yezidis, Devil Worshippers, of Kurdish not of Arab race, while in the plains to the north Arab tribes, Shammar, Tai and the rest, resume their sway.

No more wonderful natural feature exists than that which greets the eye of the traveller as he approaches the mountian wall of Kurdistan from the south. Behind him lies a universe of level lands.

But for the Jabal Sinjar, not a salient point
has broken the long expanse from the head of the
Persian Gulf. An almost imperceptible upword
slope does nothing to prepare him for the high retreats which lie behind the heat haze, and suddenly
he lifts his eyes and sees Mardin perched half way
up the heavens. Refuge and sanctuary—alas, how
often violated—for vanquished race and struggling
creed, the northern hills have been for many thousand years. Sheltered in their folds are fragments
of ancient peoples still practising strange cults
the origin of which they do not know. Here
Christianity found an early foothold ; the monks
of Basil carved out their cave cells in precipitous
rocks, and until the last massacres wiped out not
only the Armenians but all other Christian sects, as
there can be little doubt has frequently occurred,
large communities of the Syrian Church worshipped
in very ancient shrines which are scattered through
the inaccessible uplands of the Tur 'Abdin, west
to Mardin, and north to Sairt; while the indomit-
able Nestorians, Protestant in faith before any
protest had arisen in Europe, held their own to the
south of Lake Van.

Beyond Diyarbakir (the racial line is a wavering
one, for the inhabitants of Urfah to the S. W. are

mainly Turkish) Anatolia is the land of the Turk, not indeed exclusively, for, as has been said, Armenians and Greeks are numerous and the Kurdish tribes are still, as they were in Xenophon's day, predominant in the mountains on either side of the Turco-Persian Frontiers. Nevertheless the high Anatolian plateau is the home of the Turanian peasantry, half-nomadic Turkomans, Afshars and Yuruks, their cultivated fields clustered round the villages on the plateau and their summer pasturages high up in the hills where, until August, a snow wreath may be found in sheltered places. In the central area of the lakes and in the valleys which feed Maeander, Hermus, Sangarius and Halys, the wood-built hamlets hidden in thickets of fruit trees, with the poplar standing sentinel above them, are part Greek and part Turkish, and before the war the Greeks were everywhere present, pursuing impartially the career of trader or of brigand, as you passed through legend-haunted mountains to sea.

Writing now in Baghdad the vision of fair coasts and spacious uplands rises fresh in the memory; spring mornings when the white petals of fruit blossom were strewn over the shining ways of travel, blazing summer noondays and a Turkoman

cottage offering rest and refreshment in the heat
of the plains. But behind the irresponsible enjoyment of exquisite scene and courteous welcome
lies the impression of a derelict land. Though
nature has been prodigal of gifts, 500 years of
Turkish rule have brought forth no good work of
man, but over Anatolia has hung the shadow of
religious strife, deepened since the war began by
the vengeance which Turko-German rulers have
dealt out to a helpless people.

Let me return to the kindly inaffectual Turk as
I knew him and as I saw him last a prisoner. It was
in Basrah, immediately after the first great victories of our armies at Kut. A number of wounded
of Turkish soldiers, captured at Sunnai'at were
lying in one of our hospitals on the Shatt-al-Arab,
and there I visited them, summoning broken
phrases of Turkish to ask them how long they had
been in arms and whence they came. All were
Anatolian Turks, one from Caesarea, another
from Smyrna, a third from Konia, a fourth from
Eskisheher on the edge of the Phrygian hills—
"Giuzel Memlaket" they sighed "a fair province,"
and smiled again when I joined in praise.
" Janum, neh yapalum?" "what's the odds, soul of
mine?" and they wagged their bandaged heads and

reached out for another cigarette. War was over for them—neh yapalum ?

Here were the very men who have neither known how to guide their own destinies nor the fate of those subject to them in the paths of peace. Under their rule Mesopotamia, which played until the close of the Abbasid period so great a part in the history of the world, has sunk into oblivion, and Asia Minor has fallen into ruin. The words of their own scriptures shall be applied to them—and who shall say applied injustly ?—" Thus have we dispossessed them thereof and given their possessions for an inheritance with another people."

Arab Provinces—Baghdad.

FIVE years ago if I had been writing a description of the Arab provinces of Turkey I should undoubtedly have begun with Syria ; since the British occupation of the 'Iraq it is equally obvious to begin with Baghdad, not for the purpose of celebrating our victory, but because Syria is still a captive while Baghdad has been set free. No one can mistake the atmosphere that reigns here. Expectation, hope, mingled with a certain dissatisfaction, no doubt, with peremptory military metthods and complaints that civil government cannot at once be set on foot, but all borne on the breath of a heartfelt sigh of relief. Whatever may be our mistakes and shortcomings, it will be some time before the recollection of two and a half years of grinding Turkish oppression fades from the mind of men whose life and property were daily threatened. The policy pursued towards the Arabs by the Committee of Union and Progress during the war can have been dictated only by despair of reconciling the leaders of Arab thought, combined with a blind confidence in the power of the Turk to crush the subject race. In the last particular the Committee was not far from the truth ; the Arabs were indeed impotent, being unarmed and unorganized, and they are still paying the price of submission. Scarcely one of the great families of Baghdad who have made us welcome but has half a dozen of its members with the Turks—a son in the ranks of the Ottoman army on the Persian frontier, another at Mosul, a brother in Constantinople, and so forth. That few went willingly is undeniable. Rich men spent great sums in bribes to save their nearest relations from military service, but after being mulcted by Khalil and his crew, another turn was given to the screw and the young men were forced to go. Some of the most distinguished among the notables of the city were banished to Anatolia or to Constantinople, some, more fortunate, sought refuge with the tribes or remained hidden among the peasants on their estates, to return radiant when the Ottoman army had been driven out. What with the dispersal of families and the complete ignorance which must prevail as to the fate of those who are with the enemy, the cloud of war still rests upon Baghdad, hanging most heavily over the noblest heads. For the sons of famous houses think it shame to desert, even from a detested service, and the one hope left is that they may fall honourably as prisoners into British hands.

Let those who are not acquainted with the conditions throw the first stone. We on the spot have heard too much of what passed to attribute blame. Daily we see men who have not yet recovered from the effects of a prolonged anxiety. Men of intellectual distinction who had no love for Turkish institutions, and hoped for relief from the British advance, were yet induced by their fears to speak and write against the infidel aggressor. With one who had not lent his pen to Turkish uses, I was discussing shortly after my arrival in Baghdad the sudden changes of front which I had witnessed. My interlocutor was a man of exceptional independence of character, with a trenchant tongue which had placed him before our arrival in considerable jeopardy. As he rose to go I said : "There are not many things of which you stand in fear." He answered gravely : "God forbid ! I am afraid of tyranny."

The torture to which the Arab race has been submitted—I fear it cannot end wholly save with the withdrawal of Turkey from the war—was brought home to me while I was still at Basrah. The occasion was a visit to the wounded prisoners in our hospitals. Among the Turkish officers there was a young Arab who was dying of a terrible gun

shot wound in the lungs. The others, lightly
wounded, laughed and joked round him, and when I
asked if there were any who spoke Arabic, pointed
at him carelessly and answered: "There's an Arab
if you want one." The boy opened his eyes when
he heard the sound of his own tongue and in a
whisper he told me his parentage—he came of a
respectable Baghdad family. Then pulling himself
together he muttered with difficult breath, "Give
me news of the Sharif." I told him that all was
well with the Arab cause in the Hijaz. "Are you
in agreement with him?" he asked, and I answered, "There is an alliance between us." He prais-
ed God and his words sounded like a *Nunc Dimittis*.
I said : "How did they treat you Arabs in
their midst ? " His eyes grew bright with anger :
" Like dogs," he replied, " Wallah like dirt."

While such sentiments as these are so clearly
apparent and so widely spread it seems an inex-
plicable contradiction that Arab tribes should
still be fighting on the side of the Turks. Again
it is only by an impartial survey of actual conditions that the Arab point of view can be understood. To the Arab tribes the war is a visitation
from Providence with which they have no direct
concern. They have been caught in the clash

of mighty forces, the relative power of which they cannot gauge, and like some small beast which finds itself unexpectedly on the face of a gigantic anvil, they hurry blindly this way and that to escape the blows of the hammer. To preserve a whole skin is their chief concern. True, the Turks were bad masters, but who shall say that the English will in the end be better? Their experience of contending armies is that there is little to choose between them. Both trample corn fields and are as likely as not to burn tents and requisition flocks. At least the Turks are Mohammedans and have not failed to make a very potent appeal to their religious prejudices. Also for the time being they are pouring out gold among the tribes, and together with the gold they impart blood curdling warnings concerning the dire results which will ensue if the Infidel takes possession of the land. They have been masters here for generations—shall their word have no weight? It is all, as you might say, a toss up, but the toss is made with a piece of Turkish gold, judiciously weighted. We have, however, a record of two years administration in the Basrah vilayet and it is satisfactory to

note that the tribes who have come in to us have
proved loyal.

In Baghdad we are living through an emotional
hour. The peasants in the fields stop to throw
you a greeting as you pass, fruit carriers trotting
into market with their wares answer your good-
day with an invitation to dip your hand into
their baskets and eat at will, children give you a
smiling salute. The higher ranks of society are as
out-going in their own fashion and they have
more than fruit and smiles to offer. Baghdad
is the centre of a considerable intellectual activity.
Men live here whose names are renowned as
writers and as poets throughout the Arab world.
They do not easily consort with strangers, but
like mediæval scholars dwell apart and spin
their interminable Oriental lore through volume
after volume. At this moment you may come
and go in their houses and they will frequent
yours ; friendships are contracted which will not
be forgotten by either side and a basis of confidence can be established. And if to the Occidental these authors of many tomes may seem to be
linked to fame with ropes of sand, that it is not
the estimate of their country men. They have
influence ; their approval is an unquestioned

passport in Islam, it will open doors in distant places where mild Learning sits in wrapt self-contemplation, give you the freedom of what the East appreciates as good company, condone your errors and whitewash your crudities.

One sure key to the heart of these recluses is the interest which the European archæologist takes in their ancient buildings. I will not say that the satisfaction aroused is wholly historic and artistic. There is a subsidiary hope that the better administration of pious endowments will serve not only to keep the buildings from decay, but will also rehabilitate financially the professors who sit with their pupils in the delapidated upper chambers ; but there is also gratification that such monuments of 14th century Arab architecture as are left in Baghdad shall not be allowed to disappear. "The Turks on purpose suffered our mosques to decay," said the reverend guardian of the Marjaniyah, that treasury of exquisite cut brick inscriptions, "But with the aid of the high Government of the Great Britain—." The mosque itself is untouched save that half the bricks of an inscription that crowned the arch of the liwan in the courtyard have been carried to Berlin during the war. We should insist on their restoration that there may remain one perfect example of mediæval Arab art in the Eastern capital.

Broken, sunken, with ragged streets where the Turks cut thoroughfares through the town, but unspoilt by the vulgarities of Europe and the grimaces of the Levant, Baghdad lies in our hands as a trust and an opportunity, to grow, if we will, into a splendid example of modern Arab civilization. A school of architects, skilled alike in structural methods and in decoration, has never ceased to exist here ; except for the British Residency—an egregious structure—all modern buildings bear a distinctive local stamp. And greatest of all assets, Baghdad, unlike Cairo, stands on the river, which running through its midst gives space and dignity to the plan of the city.

It is the metropolis of a district rich in racial and political interest. To the east, a two days' stage— a few hours' journey in a motor car—brings you into Kurdish tribes which offer an agreeable tang of difference from their Arab neighbours. There are no prohibitive social barriers between the two peoples, but they complement rather than resemble one another. The shrines at Karbala, Najaf, Kadhimain, and Samarra, sacred centres of Shiah devotion, attract great numbers of Persian and Indian residents and pilgrims, while the Qadiriyah, in Baghdad itself, is visited by Sunnis from all parts, more especially from the Indian frontier. There is movement in the atmosphere, and those who value the Oriental mentality will not regret that Baghdad should have held so firmly to its Asiatic relationships.

The astounding fertility of the province has to a certain extent defied even Ottoman mismanagement, but on the Tigris and Diyalah cultivation extends little beyond the river banks and the prodigious wealth of the Euphrates awaits in like manner a scientific system of irrigation. The rivers left to their own devices, silt up existing canals, carve out new outlets, and when these are not sufficient lay large areas under flood. The irresponsible methods of the Arabs themselves are at the bottom of much of the mischief. No sooner does the water scour a fresh course than the cultivator with his spade sets to work to destroy it, and in his eagerness to distribute the beneficient flow uses the best of his efforts to help the channel to disappear. On the Euphrates the alterations in the two branches, the Hillah and the Hindiyah channels, have thrown the cultivated areas into confusion

During the years which preceded the building of the
Hindiyah dam by Messrs. Jackson, the old Euphrates, which runs past Hillah, had almost dried
up. Hillah itself depended on well-water during
the summer, and on the lower course of the river
the palm gardens had withered and the mud
villages were deserted. The half-settled tribesmen
moved across to the Hindiyah, with an accompanying social dislocation which it is difficult to picture.
With the building of the dam on the Hindiyah, part
of the water flowed back into the Hillah channel
and the tribesmen began to return to their former
seat ; but at the outbreak of war Turkish administration, miserably inefficient at best, vanished
entirely, the breaking of dykes has dissipated the
water and the wealth-giving flood which should be
irrigating the lower rice fields lies in a vast lake over
the desert to the west of Baghdad. A fresh scat-
tering of tribal husbandmen has been the result.
Every Shaikh who comes in to pay his respects
to the new rulers, and incidentally to receive from
them the gifts which rewards his first visit, has
the same request to proffer—water, the gift of gifts,
which shall enable him to raise abundant crops,
to bring back his vagrant tribesmen and to provide
them with an assured livelihood, with the help

and support of the Great Government and of God
Almighty. And in truth their aspirations are
entirely in accordance with the wishes of the Great
Government, except that the latter is not so exclusively concerned with the interests of Ibn So
and So as he is himself, but couple with him his
compeers along the rivers. For what other end can
be of more importance to any Government than the
settlement of the land, the provision of peaceful
and profitable work which shall check the wandering tendencies of the tribes and leave them no
leisure to pick quarrels with their neighbours—
and little motive, since intertribal differences arose
chiefly out of disputes over land and water—while
at the same time they will be turned into active
agents for the correction of one of the gravest
dangers which arises from universal war, namely a
universal shortage of food.

The Arab is essentially a money-maker. With
the utmost frankness he will tell you that greed
is the most powerful motive of his actions. But
he is also a money-spender. He likes to live well
and to go richly clad ; he clamours for the benefits
and comforts of civilization, not only material
but intellectual, and will demand educational
facilities with almost the same breath with which

he expresses his desire for silk robes and tinned pine-apples. His greed makes him anxious to exploit the natural advantages of his country. Oil pumps and modern agricultural instruments, provided that they are suited to his requirements, will all find a ready market, and the enterprising trading houses of Baghdad, mainly Jews and Christians, who even before the war had established branches in Europe, will turn their energies to supplying the wants of the country districts as soon as transport for importing goods is available. What we desire in Baghdad is the earliest opportunity for setting the ball of commerce rolling. With a population which will instantly raise its standard of living and a soil the undeveloped resources of which are ample to provide for enhanced requirements, our economic future need cause no anxiety.

Let the Great Government bear in mind that, except for Turkish neglect, a constant feature even in time of peace, Mesopotamia has suffered little if any material damage from the war. Nowhere will the traces of battle be more speedily effaced ; there were no permanent structures to destroy and there are therefore none to replace. When I came up the Tigris not a month had elapsed since heroic contests had surged round Kut, but already the signs of strife were almost obliterated. Quick-growing weeds had covered the trenches ; along the river banks where the Turkish army had fled in wild disorder with our forces at their heels, the Arabs had pitched their black tents in the accustomed camping grounds, sheep cropped the grass and buffaloes basked in the shallow water. Kut itself, tragic little monument of defeat and victory,—it stood shadowy among its riven palms as we passed it before daybreak—will in a few weeks' time be rebuilt, repeopled and summoned to new and richer life. So with the whole land of Mesopotamia— may the omen of Kut be blessed. Nowhere in the war-shattered universe can we begin more speedily to make good the immense losses sustained by humanity.

Arab Provinces—The Two Rivers.

ABOVE the latitude of Baghdad, Mesopotamia undergoes a radical change. The limits of the alluvial delta are reached some 60 miles to the north and the rivers, instead of pursuing a tortuous course through a wide expanse of deep rich soil, flow by comparatively narrow but on the whole less winding valleys, which are cut through a hard steppe of conglomerate or limestone. There are belts of alluvial deposit in the valleys, but on the steppe the layer of soil which covers the essential rock is thin. At no time has there been continuous cultivation between the rivers or in the Syrian Desert to the west of the Euphrates, although between Hit and Palmyra there are traces of permanent settlements dating back to a period not later than the beginning of our era, rude fortified cities, stone built, which drew their water from innumerable wells, now mostly blocked with earth and rubbish. A certain amount of cultivation may have existed round such places, as well as in the Wadi Hauran, which drains the Southern Syrian Desert, but the insufficiency alike of rainfall and of ground water must have precluded extensive agriculture.

The Tigris basin is singularly arid for 150 miles and more north of Samarra, but the Lesser Zab flows through a fertile district. From its mouth northwards the Tigris valley widens out and in good years the ancient city mounds of Ashur and Calah rise out of extensive cornfields. The cultivators here are semi-nomadic riverain tribes, like the Jubur and such small fry—small not in number but in political and social importance. Above Nineveh, the modern Mosul, the wealth of Assyria begins ; the flowering grass brushes your stirrup as you ride through the Kurdish foot hills, and the mountain streams cleave their way through narrow gorges where the poplar, the walnut and the plane dispute every foot of ground with fruit trees, vines and grain crops.

The Euphrates is more fertile than the Tigris. The palm grows freely as far north as 'Anah, both on the banks and in midstream, on islands which bear trace of having been very ancient settlements. Rich patches of cornland lie along the valley which would be more widely cultivated but for the depredations of the nomads. Below Dair-al-Zor there is another belt of bountiful fertility and the basins of the two eastern affluents, the Khabur and the Bilikh, are capable of great development. Where the Euphrates issues from Anti Taurus, so near to the Mediterranean that it might well have chosen that sea into which to empty itself, the plains on either side were once vast granaries which made the fortune of famous cities, the Hittite capital of Karchemish, Hierapolis, the shrine of the Syrian Goddess, Carrhae, marked by the ruin fields of Harran, and Odessa the modern Urfah. How lively were the anticipations of gain when these northern districts should be rendered accessible by the Baghdad railway was proved by the fact that four years ago, when railhead was drawing near the Euphrates at Karchemish enterprizing Arab capitalists of Damascus and Basrah had bought up much of the land on the upper tributaries of the Jaghjaghah, east of Nisibin, and were congratulating themselves on the profits which would accrue to them when they could carry their corn by rail down to the sea at Alexandretta. The rainfall here is sufficient in good years for the raising of crops without artificial irrigation, and this is true also of the fertile district east of the Tigris, of which Arbela may be said to be the centre and the Lower Zab the southern boundary.

Between the rivers, from Baghdad northwards
to the Khabur and the Jabal Sinjar, the open
steppe is inhabited by nomad Arabs who neither
sow nor harvest, and they occupy the whole
desert between the Euphrates and Syria. The
history of these confederations, as far as it can be
pieced together, is governed by a factor which
from the earliest days has dominated Arabia, the
unbroken drift northwards of the peoples of the
peninsula. The underlying causes of the movement were probably complex. A gradual change
in climatic conditions involving slow dessication,
the pressure of an increasing population on a soil
growing ever poorer, and the opportunities of
northern expansion offered by the weakness or
political exhaustion of neighbouring northern
States being the most weighty. The earliest
migrations Semiticised Babylonia and colonized
Assyria; another pulsation established Arab
authority in and round Damascus, and the Mohammedan invasion was but one of many similar
phenomena. It is not until close upon the Mohammedan era that we begin to take cognizance of
tribal groups which are still in existence. These
early comers must be sought, however, not among
the true Beduin of to-day in the central Meso-

potamian plains and the Syrian Desert, regions which they were forced to relinquish to stronger hordes from the south. The old tribes exist on the edges of the area of immigration, where they are to be found half-settled and forced to till the soil for want of the wide spaces necessary for nomadic life. Thus the Qais and the Mawali are dwellers in villages on the furthest confines of Mesopotamia. The Tai, whose fame was so great in the early middle ages that their name represented in further Asia the whole nomad Arabian nation, share the extreme north-eastern pasturages with Kurdish tribes. Not infrequently the groups have been split up and separated by intruding confederations. The Zubaid, one of the most powerful tribes of northern 'Iraq, are also noted highwaymen in the desert south-east of Damascus.

The tribesmen have preserved some memory of their origin and history, the general outline of which is usually correct, so far as it can be submitted to proof. There is, for instance, a very old community called the Bani Tamim, well known in pre-Mohammedan traditions, concerning whom it is certain that in the 5th century they occupied the whole of Central Arabia. The

majority of the oasis dwellers of Najd are to-day
Bani Tamim, but an important migration to
Mesopotamia occurred about the Mohammedan
era and sections of the tribe are scattered through
the 'Iraq and in the plains below the Persian hills.
One of the 'Iraq Shaikhs came in to pay his
respects shortly after the occupation of Baghdad
and in the course of conversation I asked him
whether he held any intercourse with his distant
relations in Najd. He answered : " Not long
since there came a man of the Bani Tamim from
Najd seeking for his kin. He went to the Bani
Tamim in the Hawizah, and to those on the
'Adhaim, and to the Shaikhs on the Tigris, but
he could not satisfy himself that they were those
whom he sought. And at last he came to us
in the Aqar Quf " (it is a district to the west of
Baghdad) " and we entertained him. And he
asked us, ' What is your wasm, your camel
brand ? ' We answered, ' Our wasm is a bar and
a circle.' Then he rejoiced and said, ' That is
my wasm also and you are my kindred'. But
we had not met for generations. And he wonder-
ed to find us Shi'ahs, they being all Wahhabis
in Najd. Dunya ! Such is the world " observed
the Shaikh, tacitly accepting the axiom that faith
is determined by environment.

The Beduin who now roam the northern wildernesses did not begin to make their appearance
until the middle of the 17th century when a large
section of the Shammar from northern Central
Arabia pressed up into the Syrian Desert, driving
the older tribal population before them. The
'Anazah followed close upon the heels of the
Shammar, forced the latter across Euphrates into
Northern Mesopotamia, and occupying the whole
of the Syrian Desert as far north as Aleppo.
They have themselves crossed the northern
reaches of the Euphrates and have appropriated
the pasturages between the Khabur and the
Bilikh. These two confederations dictate the
tribal politics of the two rivers. A secular hostility to one another is the guiding principle of
their actions, raid and counter-raid across the
Euphrates or the Khabur the sum of their relations
with each other. The Turk has never succeeded
in holding them. An occasional *coup de main*,
resembling one of their own forays rather than
the exercise of paramount sovereignty, has checked
from time to time some particularly turbulent
chief. A large resort has been made by Ottoman
officials to treacherous overtures and false promises, but the tribes have contrived to wriggle

out of permanent obedience and, safe within their
own deserts, have mocked at Turkish rule. Like
all nomads they are dependent on the settled
lands for foodstuffs and on the towns for clothes
and utensils, not to speak of such essential luxuries
as coffee and tobacco. A firm and judicious
administration should therefore have little difficulty in controlling them. Left to himself the
idle hungry Bedawi, picturesque figure as he
undoubtedly is and romantic social asset, is the
ban of civilisation. He is the marauder whose
lawless depredations must be bought off since
there has been no power capable of restraining
them. His private interests run counter to those
of the community. He does not wish to see the
plough conquer fresh acres where the wild herbs
were enough for his sheep and camels, nor the
highroads where he waylaid merchant and mule-
teer, held up the post and put the traveller to
ransome, turned into secure and well guarded
ways of communication and commerce. Peace
does not suit him ; he has not the smallest inclin-
ation to set a term to blood feuds which combine
pleasurable excitement with the fulfilment of
family duties. But these predilections, though
they are strongly rooted, are not invincible. The

cultivating tribes along the rivers, who were
nomadic a couple of hundred years ago, are now
villagers under a tribal organization, and some
of the great Shaikhs of the Beduin have recognized
the solid advantage of real property, and though
they still boast that they are unfettered children
of the wilderness, are in fact anchored by the
possession of estates and gardens in the settled
areas. Thus Fahad Beg ibn Hadhdhal, paramount
Shaikh of the eastern 'Anazah, a man whose pru-
dence and wisdom combined with his high descent
have earned him the respect of the whole desert
from the Euphrates to Damascus—he has been
our honoured guest in Baghdad—owns property
on the Husainiyah canal west of Karbala and can
produce Turkish title deeds by which he sets
great store. There can be no question that the
process of settlement would have been accelerated
if a policy different from that of the Porte had
been applied to the tribes. Greed, the national
characteristic, sways the Bedawi just as much as it
influences his brother in the rice fields of 'Iraq,
but Ottoman maladministration offered too little
inducement to money making, while the one
thing which was incontrovertible was that the
moment you took to living permanently at any

spot accessible to Ottoman officials you would be
subject to their extortions. Moreover the dread
of military service was a convincing deterrent.

There is no trace of settled habitation in the
steppe between the rivers until you reach the
Khabur, where Layard found remains of Assyrian
cities. To the east the prodigious ruins of the
Parthian Hatra, three times vainly besieged by
Roman armies, rise from the grass grown levels.
In decay it is still a desert capital, for the great
Shaikhs of the Shammar regard it as their own
and pitch their tents in spring round its palaces.
When I camped there in 1911 it was occupied
by a Turkish Brigade which had been despatched
thither by Nizam Pasha, Vali of Baghdad, to
collect taxes long overdue on sheep and camels—
the last occasion, to the best of my knowledge,
on which they have been accorded by the tribe.
The wells at Hatra are now and have probably
always been extremely brackish. About a mile
from the city walls run the bitter waters of the
Tharthar, a stream fed from the Jabal Sinjar.
It pursues a course more or less parallel to the
Tigris till it empties itself into the marshes north
of Aqar Quf. It is mentioned in a remarkable
cuneiform record left by an early Assyrian monarch

who carried out a great raid from Ashur with the intention of pillaging Babylon, but found the latter too big a nut to crack and contented himself with a booty-seeking return journey along the Euphrates and Khabur. The Tharthar was in his day as salt as it is at present, that is to say barely drinkable, for he relates how his army came to the valley and all night drew water, but for the king sweet water was carried from the Tigris.

A long two days' ride north from Hatra brings you to the Jabal Sinjar where first you come into contact with a race which is non-Arab. The Sinjar hills are the stronghold of the Yazidis, an untamed people who are the terror of the Arab tribes as far as the Euphrates. Concerning their origin the learned disagree. They speak Kurdish, their Shaikhly family north-east of Mosul, where their principal shrine is situated, claim descent from the Arab tribe of Tai; some men say that they are an Armenian race, though they have not the physical characteristics, some say that they are Jews, and God knows best. The shrine at Shaikh 'Adi in the mountains above Mosul, is a small mosque-like building, frequently destroyed, with a black snake and other strange decorations carved about the door, but the symbol of their faith is the Sacred Peacock which represents the Devil himself. The name "Devil Worshippers" by which the Yezidis are known to us, has too sinister a ring; they do not worship, but merely propitiate the Power of Evil. Whatever may be their tenets, Christendom is in their debt. Since the outbreak of war the Yezidis have thrown off the Turkish yoke and they are now sheltering in their rocky hills several thousand Armenian women and children whom they rescued from the hands of the Turks in the deserts south of Nisibin. For those who know the history of the Yezidis there is a wonderfully significant note in this act of humanity. Like all small sects who have been obliged to guard their rites by veiling them in secrecy and have thereby incurred charges of hidden evil, the Yezidis have suffered a long-sustained persecution at the hands of their neighbours, Moslem and Christian alike. Time out of number the "Devil Worshippers" have been slaughtered like sheep in their mountain villages or driven down into the plains to find death or worse awaiting them, and it was their own experience of Ottoman brutality which lay behind the generous onset that liberated the Armenian women. Nor do they afford a solitary example of the rising of the persecuted to rescue the persecuted. The Qizil Bash, in central Anatolia, have come to the help of the Armenians in similar fashion and hold a number of them safe in their impenetrable valleys.

The pity and indignation roused by the agony of the Armenian race has done its work. All sects have been moved by the sight of such unimagined cruelty, and Moslems vie with Christians in expressions of abhorrence. It must not be forgotten that there was no persecution of the Armenians in the Arab provinces, and indeed there is little or no fanaticism among Arab Mohammedans. Individual cases of violent feeling may occur, just as a few wild tribes may be stirred by the cry of Holy War, but there is no Arab town or district in which Moslems and Christians do not live in unity, if not in friendship. The Moslem is the ruler and claims his privilege, but he confines it within reasonable limits. In Baghdad and Damascus the Armenians were never threatened, and though in the latter town the Turks sold Armenian women openly in the public market, in Baghdad the handful of girls who found their way down from the north were taken into Moslem houses and kindly treated till we came and made provision for them.

In briefest outline such is the land of the two rivers, an Arab country except for the Kurdish tribes upon its eastern frontier, a land of pasture with rich belts of cultivation along the streams and extensive arable tracts to the north, as well as in the Kurdish foot hills to the east. Mesopotamia is essentially the domain of the shepherd and the ploughman. Its mineral wealth is comparatively of little importance. The bitumen wells at Hit, famous since the days of the Babylonians, with their accompanying sulph ur springs; petroleum wells of indifferent quality at Qayyarah, south of Mosul—no doubt connected with the inexhaustible subterranean petroleum lake of south-west Persia—good stone quarries on the Euphrates below 'Anah, a little coal in the Jabal Hamrin and the salt of the Wadi Tharthar, make pretty nearly the sum of exploited minerals. It is not necessary to plunge beneath the soil to find riches ; the depth of a ploughshare is enough.

Arab Provinces—Syria.

I MUST write of Syria as I knew it, though my recollections can, I fear, bear little resemblance to the Syria of to-day. When the Turk has been driven from Damascus and Aleppo we shall learn in detail the results of Jamal Pasha's savage rule, but already we have heard enough to know that Syria is now the worn shadow of what she was. I cannot think of this desolation without a seething anger and a desire for vengeance on Turk and German which few of their abominable deeds have succeeded in rousing. From south to north, from the desert borders of Arabia to Anti Taurus, I know the pleasant Syrian country and have received at the hands of its inhabitants, Mohammedan, Jew, Christian, Druze, Nosairi, whatever may be their cult, hospitable welcome, service and kindness. With many of them it has been more than a passing acquaintance. Friendship has grown up between us, a friendship which was renewed from year to year, so that to return to Damascus or to Aleppo was to drop back into a familiar circle. The fate of those who bore names so distinguished that they could not disappear unnoticed has been published in the Turkish newspapers. Not one in twenty has been left alive. They were condemned to death by Jamal's bloody tribunal in the Lebanon, or sent with their families into unspecified exile in Asia Minor, whence it is improbable that they will ever return. Some few have made their way to Egypt or crossed the desert to claim our protection in Baṣrah, and concerning this handful only can we be certain that they have escaped the fury of the Turk. As for the humbler, but no less esteemed companions of many journeys, servants, muleteers and camel drivers, they must have shared the common fate of the peasant population. The younger men have been impressed into the Turkish Army, the older men driven into labour corps, to die of hard work and starvation under Ottoman task-masters. And their women folk, the wives and mothers who spread out their best for us when we came travel-stained home, have endured a destiny no less tragic.

The reason of the extreme violence of the Committee of Union and Progress towards Syria is not far to seek, nor, from the Turko-German point of view, is it unjustifiable. Syria was the brain of modern Arab civilization, the birth-place of the Arab movement and the link between the eastern and the extreme western provinces, Mesopotamia and North Africa. Its geographical position had put it closely into touch with European political thought, the yearly influx of tourists to the Holy Land and Damascus gave Europeans a sentimental interest in the country and people, and the fact that the Lebanon was administered under an International guarantee involved the Powers in responsibilities which they could not disclaim. The Committee was thus face to face with conditions peculiarly abhorrent; the party which asked for decentralization on racial ground was stronger in Syria than elsewhere, and the protest of Europe was more likely to attend high-handed action on the part of the Ottoman Government. The outbreak of war cut the knot. Germany would not raise objections to the persecution of Arabs any more than she objected to the massacre of Armenians. The golden opportunity for cowing the Arab race, unhindered by foreign intervention, had arrived, and Turk and German turned to hacking their way through the life of a nation. The Arabs were not prepared to offer resistance. The fatal lack of cohesion, inherent in a society which has never succeeded in obliterating its tribal origins, had run counter to any national union. At best there was little more than what may be described as municipal patriotism, a unity which extended no further than the limits of the big townships. Comprehensive organization was non-existent and the country yielded without striking a blow.

It must be admitted that the elements which make up the population of Syria are peculiarly varied, not to say incongruous. West of Jordon the clash of religious jealousy, even if it has ceased to be vitally disruptive, East of Jordan the disintegrating influence of tribal authority forbid the development of a true national sentiment. From Damascus northward a greater homogeneity prevails but even here each separate religious sect, Mohammedans, Christians of every pattern, Nosairis, or down-trodden Ismailis, revolves round its own axis and regards as comparatively unimportant its connection with the system of which it forms a part.

Not least among the denationalizing forces is the fact that a part of Syria, though like the rest mainly inhabited by Arabs, is regarded by a non-Arab people as its prescriptive inheritance. At a liberal estimate the Jews of Palestine may form a quarter of the population of the province, the Christians a fifth, while the remainder are

Mohammedan Arabs. Jewish immigration has been artificially fostered by doles and subventions from millionaire co-religionists in Europe; the new colonies have now taken root and are more or less self-supporting. The pious hope that an independent Jewish state may some day be established in Palestine no doubt exists, though it may be questioned whether among local Jews there is any acute desire to see it realized, except as a means of escape from Turkish oppression; it is perhaps more lively in the breasts of those who live far from the rocky Palestinian hills and have no intention of changing their domicile. Lord Cromer took pleasure in relating a conversation which he had held on the subject with one of the best known English Jews, who observed: "If a Jewish Kingdom were to be established at Jerusalem I should lose no time in applying for the post of Ambassador in London." Apart from the prevalence of such sentiments two considerations rule out the conception of an independent Jewish Palestine from practical politics. The first is that the province as we know it is not Jewish, and that neither Mohammedan nor Arab would accept Jewish authority; the second that the capital, Jerusalem, is equally sacred to three faiths, Jewish,

Christian and Moslem, and should never, if it can be avoided, be put under the exclusive control of any one local faction, no matter how carefully the rights of the other two may be safeguarded.

Whether or no it could be turned into a fitting home for millionaires, for the lover of simple things Palestine has a singular attraction. Grey limestone rocks, grey-green olive groves coloured like a precious celadon dish, upland vineyards haunted still by little foxes, and in the steep valleys, rocky crevices full to the brim with starch hyacinths, cypripedium, anemone and cyclamen On the sea coast flourish the orange groves which have made the fame of Jaffa, while inland the barren wilderness of Judaea drops abruptly into the cornlands and hot-house temperatures of the Jordan valley. The wealth of the mountain country, that is to say of the greater part of Palestine, is of vine, olive and corn ; there is no other.

Across Jordan lies the best of Syria, to my thinking, Edom and Moab to the south, Gilead to the north. The desert sweeps in close to the abrupt declivities which form a cup for the Dead Sea, but it is a desert which has no parallel elsewhere, a rolling pasturage abandoned only for a few months in the summer by the camel herds of the Beduin and the flocks of half settled tribes. Sturdy farmers, many of them Christian —the most virile of the Christians of Syria except those of Aleppo—have pushed their cornfields into the margins of the grass-lands, to the farthest limits of profitable husbandry and to the last outposts of ancient habitation. But beyond the track of the plough and the ruins of villages pre-Mohammedan and probably largely pre-Christian, are the massive remains of a girdle of Roman fortresses, the Limites of Trajan, Septimius Severus and Diocletian, and yet further east the carved and frescoed hunting lodges of the Umayyad Khalifs of Damascus serve as shelter to the nomad shepherd. The Christians of these parts come from Madeba above the Dead Sea, and from Salt, a little town lying among fruit gardens on the southern edge of Gilead—its inhabitants boast that their ancestors received the faith from the very lips of its Founder. They have held their own against the exactions of the Government on the one hand and the blackmail of the tribes on the other. They are obliged to keep open house for the tribes in their farms on the borders of the desert, and not a night passes without the guest chamber being filled with ragged Arabs and the stables with their mares, while for man and beast a liberal meal must be provided. These unwelcome guests eat most of the profits of the farms, but if they were refused hospitality they would make all industry impossible by raid and foray which the Government neither could nor would control.

In the heart of Gilead there is a large Circassian colony, the head-quarters of which is the ancient Raboth Ammon, a town which, like the neighbouring Jarash, must have been a luxurious seat of civilization at the beginning of our era. The remains of a huge theatre tower above the modern Government offices, the niched walls of a Nympheum adorn the banks of the stream, and latest of all splendours, a beautiful Umyyad building crowns the hill top. The thrifty Circassians have planted trees and laid out gardens down the valley, the stream turns their sawmill, and their two wheeled carts creak over the best roads in trans-Jordan. They are not loved of their neighbours, but it may be said in their defence that a hand to hand struggle for existence does not tend to sweeten national characteristics.

East of Gilead lies the volcanic outcrop of the Hauran, inhabited by Druze immigrants from Lebanon, a race of strong men and beautiful women, practising a strange cult neither Christian nor Moslem, but rooted most probably in far older traditions than the 11th century legendary teachings of a mad Sultan of Egypt in which it is supposed to have originated. Fierce and subtle and faultlessly brave, the Druzes of the Hauran are feared by the tribes and by Turkish officials ; they have succeeded in maintaining a virtual independence of Ottoman rule, though periodical military expeditions ending in wholesale massacre have prevented the mountain people from extending their borders.

A short two days' ride from the Jabal Hauran brings you to Damascus, the pulse of modern Arab political life, capital alike of modern Arab civilization and of the ancient desert. The powerful 'Anazah nation of Beduin, who link Mesopotamia with Syria, resort to it as freely as the merchant of Beyrut, the pilgrims on his way to Mecca, and the tourist. It was, before the war, just as it was in the 7th century when the Umayyad Khalifs held their court there, the leading city of the Arab race, though the immense natural wealth of Mesopotamia may once more raise Baghdad, as it was raised in the Middle Ages, to a position surpassing even that of Damascus. I write of it as I knew it during a 15 years' acquaintance, gracious and hospitable, rich in fruit and flowers and running water, a Paradise on earth as its citizens were accustomed to declare.

The greatest of all the natural advantages which it enjoys is the proximity of mountains. The snows of Hermon are scarcely more than a day's journey distant, and the villages of Anti-Lebanon give summer retreats no less delightful, and more solitary, than the hostelries of Lebanon, which are somewhat overrun by Levantines of Beyrut and Alexandria. But the Lebanon also has its enchantments, its Maronite villages perched half way between sea and sky, its vine clad or wooded slopes with streams gushing from the rock, most famous among them the Afka spring, which is still in spate coloured red with the blood of Adonis.

It is difficult to recall now the peace and beauty of that mountain range, trailing its skirts in the blue Mediterranean. It has suffered more at Jamal's hand than any other part of Syria. Olive and fruit tree have been felled to supply fuel for

the railway, the peasants, cut off from all sources
of supply by a strict cordon, have died of hunger
or wandered starving into Beyrut to perish
there, and terrible tales are rife of children sold
by their parents, wives by their husbands, for the
price of a bag of flour.

That this appalling shortage of food must be
due in part to active measures taken by the
Turko-German authorities to starve out the Arab
people becomes more apparent as one's memories
travel north. The Orontes valley is a vast cornfield and with the wheat growing plains east of
Aleppo could supply many armies and yet leave
the inhabitants in plenty if the harvest were
equitably distributed. Homs and Hamah are
the capitals of this district, both of them towns
of great antiquity, and a yet older foundation,
the Hittite Kadish on the Orontes, remains in the
shape of a huge mound with a few Arab hovels
on its summit overlooking Lake Kattinah. Like
all the Syrian towns, Homs and Hamah have
their peculiar colour and characteristics, but they
shared in the universal well-being, the air of
prosperous ease which used to prevail in Syria.
And like Damascus they are closely in touch with
the Arab tribes, more especially the northern

'Anazah who in summer drive their cattle into
the harvested fields, with the accompanying small
disturbances which occur when the desert annu-
ally invades the settled lands. The town-bred
Syrian by long custom has grown used to them
and scarcely notices them except for a shrug of
the shoulders and a passing observation that the
Beduin are savages. But sharp as the demarcation may appear between the desert man in his
ragged shirt and black cloak, smelling of camel
and campfire, his hair hanging in plaits to the
shoulders, and the smart European-clad landowner, let us say of Hamah, the truly amazing
particular is how easily it can be overstepped. In
one generation the Beduin can be transformed
into an accomplished citizen of the world. I
knew a man who was born in the tents of a raga-
muffin little tribe which maintained a precarious
existence, by means chiefly connected with
highway robbery, in the lava belt south of Damascus. His father was Shaikh, with paramount
authority over thieves, goats and stones, but
being possessed of some breadth of mind, he
desired to see his children taught to read and write
and to that end engaged a teacher, a Christian,
who kept school in the tent next door. These

instructions, however, came to an abrupt end by
a reason of a raid by a neighbouring tribe, which
so frightened the unhappy schoolmaster that he
fled hastily and refused to return. A year or
two later the Shaikh chanced to be in Damascus
with his eldest boy. It was the moment when
the Sultan Abdul Hamid was founding in Constantinople a school for the sons of Shaikhs, with
the object of catching them young and turning
them into zealous Ottomans. Six boys had been
requisitioned from Syria and the Shaikh of the
Sulut was pressed to contribute a son. He com-
plied and my friend proceeded to Constantinople.
" Were you not surprised when you saw that
city ?" I interrupted the narrative. " Surprised !" he said. " I had been bewildered when
I set foot in Damascus ". He pursued his education with great profit to himself, but without
forwarding the original aim of his Lord the Sultan.
The Shaikhs' sons were not Ottomanized, though
all imaginable pains were taken to show them
the glory of the Turk and make them forget their
lineage and their language. They became, on
the contrary, more Arab than before and acquired
a far better understanding, as the children of
various deserts made acquaintance with one

another, of what it was to be an Arab. This acquaintance stood my friend in good stead when the day came on which he found himself obliged to flee for his life and cross the whole Mesopotamian desert from north to south to find safety with us in Basrah. In every important tribal confederation he fell in with a school fellow who held him on his way. "Have you ever returned to the tents of the Sulut ?" said I, after listening to this remarkable history. "I have been back" he said, "but they regard me as a stranger and I look on them as a pack of thieves".

Furthest north of the four great Syrian towns —for I do not reckon Levantine Beyrut, nor yet sacred and sectarian Jerusalem as truly Syrian—lies Aleppo, on the edge of Turkish speaking peoples. Its position and the long and intimate relation with the outer world which as a famous commercial centre it has enjoyed, have given a peculiar tinge to the mentality of its citizens, a cynicism born of familiarity with the universe, or at least with the Oriental universe, a certain indifference, combined with considerable individual activity, and a cheerful cosmopolitanism. I cannot picture any important religious or social reform originating at Aleppo, neither

could Alepping society be led far astray by mis-
placed enthusiasm. Incitements to massacre,
for instance, are received with polite surprise,
even when, as in 1911, Armenians were extermin-
ated in villages not a day's journey to the west.

Let me end by giving the latest description of
Aleppo which I received recently from a refugee,
for it epitomizes the Syria of Jamal. "You
cannot pass through the town," said he, "without
a contraction of the heart. In every house there
is wailing, and the streets are full of the sound
of it."

Turkish Provinces—The Kurdish Mountains.

THE Arab provinces, though they may exhibit diversity of custom and of creed, are not only generally homogeneous in race, but will probably tend, if they are allowed to pursue their natural course, towards a greater unity of aim and interest than that which they have possessed hitherto. From the Mediterranean to within a couple of days' march of the Persian frontier one language is spoken, and if the Christian communities have been accustomed to regard themselves as Christians rather than as Arabs, it must be admitted that there has been little advantage to be gained from participation in a nationality which was without political authority, or possessed it only in reflex from a Power far more definitely suspicious of Christian aspirations and hostile to any assumption of equality than ever the Arabs have shown themselves. But if to be an Arab should come to imply membership in a dominant race, it will be the interest of all inhabitants of the Arab provinces to claim their share in it. Their common origin will no longer be unappreciated and their common language will facilitate completer assimilation.

The exact contrary of these conditions prevails
in what I have called generically the Turkish
Provinces. The Turanian element of the population has over the whole of Asia Minor a bare
majority, if it has any majority at all, and in many
districts it is largely outnumbered by others. The
Turkish language has an official currency and is
everywhere familiar, but among themselves the
people speak their own tongues and hold to them.
In the phraseology of politics this diversity is
acknowledged, and in dealing with Asia Minor we
do not talk of it as Turkey pure and simple, but
consider it in fractions such as Armenia (though
Lord Salisbury acknowledged that he could not
give exact geographical definition to the term)
or Kurdistan. It may be objected that Great
Britain is similarly composite and yet presents
a united front, to which I would answer that only
in the first particular does the parallel hold good.
Diversity occurs in Asia Minor as in Great Britain,
but in Asia Minor there is no union.

Nowhere is political and racial chaos more
apparent than in Kurdistan. As I have said,
the rugged and to this day almost inaccessible
mountain ranges of southern and south-eastern
Anatolia have been the refuge of fugitives from

the plains driven out by recurrent invasions.
So the Medes pushed out the Assyrians, and the
Arab migrations, which began before the Moslem
conquest and cannot be said to have ceased completely at any date, uprooted afresh Medes,
Parthians and the yet older Semitic settlers.
Moreover the mountains have been from the
earliest historic times the seat of different races.
Xenophon found there the Kardukhi who are
the Kurds; the Armenian Kingdom goes back
to the 6th century B.C., and before it we know
dimly of political units standing in close relations
with the Hittites, concerning which it cannot
definitely be stated to what division of mankind
they belonged. These people have overlapped,
but they have not fused. Much of Kurdistan,
regarded from a different standpoint, is Armenia
—a fact which goes far to justify Lord Salisbury's ignorance—and when all historic circum-
stance is taken into account it is not surprising
to find that while there are few parts of Anatolia
where a considerable proportion of the population is not bilingual, in the southern hills men use
currently three and even four tongues. Thus in
the wild valleys north of the Greater Zab, the
principal eastern afflueunt of the Tigris above
Mosul, I have met villagers who talked Kurdish,

Arabic, and Turkish, but their own speech when conversing with one another was a Semitic dialect known as Fallahi, the Peasant Tongue, which in spite of its derogatory name is, I believe, no other than the torn remnant of ancient Assyrian. In the Tur 'Abdin, east of Mardin, the mother tongue of the Christians is Syriac, but they speak besides Kurdish and Arabic and have usually a smattering of Turkish. These conditions must be taken into account in any attempt to gauge the political solidarity of the Turkish provinces.

I have so far left out of count the Circassians, who are recent comers and comparatively few in number. Nevertheless wherever these immigrants from the Caucasus have succeeded in establishing themselves, they have introduced a wholly different and extremely vigorous racial element which has made its mark. Vigorous, indeed, it must have been in order to maintain existence against the odds which confronted it. The settlement best known to me is that of Ras al 'Ain, until recently the terminus of the Aleppo-Mosul section of the Baghdad railway. There the headman of the village, with Russian samovar ever hospitably ready to supply tea to his guests, related to me his experiences, which may (I can vouch for it) be accepted as typical of the history

of Circassian Muhajir as a whole. He was a
man over 70—this was in 1911 and he may, God
rest him, have ended before now his eventful
career. He had come down as a child into the
edges of the desert ; you can picture the flight out
of Caucasus—whole families with their cattle
and such worldly goods as they could carry
heaped on the two-wheeled carts, with the babes
atop of all. The Sultan had allotted to them
lands round the great spring which is one of the
sources of the Bilikh, but when they reached
their destination they found that the Sultan's
power to allot was of the most questionable kind,
nor was he in a position to assist them to make
good. In hand to hand combat they challenged
the rival claims of Kurd and Arab, and when they
had leisure to exchange the rifle for the plough,
by hard toil they gained a narrow livelihood.
" If the railway comes our way," said my host
(at that time the projected trace had not been
made public), " we shall prosper. Otherwise
I see no hope." " Have you ever revisited the
Caucasus ?" I enquired. " Yes," he answered,
" I went there ten years ago. Khanum Effendi,
we should not have left our country. Those who
remained have grown to be rich men ; they hold

posts under the Russian Government and have acquired lands and possessions. If we had stayed, we also should have prospered." I have heard the same from the lips of many a Circassian migrant and it is perhaps as striking a condemnation of Ottoman rule as could be cited, for it shows the Turk impotent to help those who had sacrificed everything rather than their allegiance to him.

But the Circassians in more bountiful districts than Ras al 'Ain have known how to help themselves. There remains in my memory the vivid impression made by a group of their villages east of Caesarea. We came down wooded and well-nigh pathless steeps into what was almost European rural scenery, fields carefully tilled, roads mended, rivulets bridged, cottages surrounded by a neatly fenced garden, and a well-dressed peasantry sitting on benches by the doorways in sunset relaxation from labour.

And what of those concerning whom the Turkish Government was devoid even of the desire to help? I passed through the exquisite valleys of the upper Euphrates basin a month after the Adana massacres of 1909. It was spring; there was snow on the high pass which divides the head

waters of the Tigris from the Euphrates, but the
Kharput plain, the grass lands round Malatia,
where the Sultan 'Abdul Hamid, then but lately
deposed, had instituted a large and well-found
horse-breeding farm, were a miracle of fertile
abundance. The corn was in the ear, the mulberry
trees burdened with fruit, the vines set thick
with small green bunches of grapes; the soil
shouted beauty and plenty. But in the Armenian
villages panic was scarcely laid to rest. Tales
of Adana were in every mouth; tales, too, of the
narrow margin which had lain between the speak-
ers themselves and massacre. And as I journeyed
further west I came into the skirts of destruction
and saw charred heaps of mud and stone which
had been busy centres of agricultural life. The
blow had been stayed midway. The population,
destitute and homeless, had defended itself and
come off with naked existence—a respite of six
years, if we had known it, until 1915 carried out
the work which 1909 had left uncompleted.

I have written elsewhere of the ethics of massacre and in the midst of infernal deeds, of which
the news still reaches us, I yet bear testimony
that massacre in the Turkish provinces was never
engendered from within. The order came, and

it was obeyed. But though I know this to be true, I do not urge it as an excuse. Such obedience is a crime against which humanity must defend itself or forfeit the right to live, and against a similar obedience humanity defends itself against at this hour in waging war with Germany.

So far as my knowledge goes the Kurds have shown a greater natural ferocity in their dealings with the Christians than the Turks, possibly only because they are possessed of a quicker vitality than the Turkish peasant, who exhibits more of the qualities of a heavy-witted animal answering to the goad. In the parts of Kurdistan with which I am acquainted, the Kurd was more dreaded by the Christian than was the Turk dreaded in districts predominantly Turkish. The Nestorians of Tiari, north-east of Mosul, have suffered without intermission at Kurdish hands, and though their amazing courage has preserved them from complete annihilation, the forces opposed to them have been too strong and even before the war it seemed as if they must ultimately succumb. So too the Syrian churches in the Tur 'Abdin; if they have not been crushed out of existence by the Kurdish Beys, at least all progress has been made impossible. Their monasteries, stripped

of wealth and reduced as to inmates to a hundredth
part of their mediæval glory, could not afford to
declare themselves too poor to offer hospitality
to every Kurdish party of armed men which rode
their way, though even the dry bread, eggs, oil
and raisins, which were all they could provide,
were a serious item in their pinched resources. But
before the war the monks could at least count on
life, and in their inaccessible rock-cut cells presented an exact picture of the conditions which
aided and sustained mediæval monaticism—the
possibility of finding in a lawless world some hope
of immunity from the worst ills, at the price of
service and hospitality which there were no
others to dispense. But according to reports
received, if not the worst, at least the final ill
has overtaken them, and the tiny historic communities have been blotted out.

The like has happened throughout Kurdistan.
Mardin was a shambles ; turbulent, black-avised
Diyarbakir, finest of sinister fenced cities, a raging
hell. In the days of 'Abdul Hamid—nine years
of Union and Progress rule almost persuade one
that in the future he will be remembered as
blessed—there was one Kurdish community which
prided itself on mercy towards Christians. That

strong leader of the Milli, Ibrahim Pasha, himself
by race an Arab, whatever may have been his
faults or crimes, made the country from the
Euphrates to Nisbin a sanctuary for the Christian
faith. The first year of the Committee saw his
fall, and though his sons, after long imprisonment, regained a part of his authority, they are
suspects, and indeed one of them is now a refugee
with us in Baghdad.

But the Kurds must not be judged wholly by
their relations with the Christian sects. If they
have the vices they have also many of the virtues
of a primitive civilization. The social code which
they apply to themselves has made them as
renowned for clean living as for courage, nor
have they had fewer wrongs than other nationalities under Turkish misrule. It is well to remember that in all parts of Asiatic Turkey agrarian troubles lie at the root of tribal unrest, and
this is as true of the half nomadic Kurds as of
the uneasy cultivators of Mesopotamia. Most
of the land has passed by questionable means into
the hands of wealthy Moslems who screw rack-rents
out of their tenants. The tyranny of the tribal
leaders is that of the feudal baron of mediæval
Europe. In the wildest parts the Kurdish peasan-

try are the serfs of their Shaikhs and Beys and
Aghas, and but for greater security to life are no
better off than the Christians.

In the strip of Asia Minor now in Russian hands,
the backbone of which is the ancient track by
which the Ten Thousand found their way to the
sea, the population along the coast shows a strong
admixture of Greeks. Many of the villages are
nominally Moslem, but the features of the inhabitants as well as their customs and ceremonies,
betray their Hellenic origin. Round Rizah,
east of Trebizond, are the Lazes, a Tibetan race
from the Caucasus, seamen of the Black Sea and
in faith fanatical Moslems. Savage, intolerant,
quick with the knife, the Turkish proverb gives
a rough and ready appreciation of them : of birds
the silliest is the goose, of men the worst the Laz.
Away from the coast the Greek element almost
disappears and the Armenian takes its place,
amounting before the war at Erzerum to about
50 per cent. of the population and retaining that
proportion down to Van and Bitlis. The Turks,
on the other hand, who at Erzerum form half of
the population, give place southward to the
Kurds. Round Bitlis Turks are few in number

and in some of the Kurdish villages Turkish is not understood.

The mountainous nature of the ground, the unfertile character of the soil and lack of communications have kept this country in a state of poverty. Nearly all the wood has long ago been burnt and in winter the inhabitants herd for warmth with sheep and cattle. Formerly some profit was derived from the caravans passing between Trebizond and Bitlis, but almost all this trade now goes through Batum and the Caucasus.

The whole region has been for long under the moral influence of Russia. For 200 years that Tatar wall separating it from Russia has been gradually narrowing and men are still alive who remember the Russian invasion of 1878. The feeling of the Turk has become embodied in the phrase: the Muscovite fear. Seeing what a difference there is between the condition of the Christians in the Russian Caucasus and that of their co-religionists over the Turkish border, what wonder if the feeling of the Armenians in Turkey towards the Russians was not always one of fear? Yet it would be wrong to think that the Armenian population was solidly pro-Russian. There were plenty of young Armenian bloods who worked in a futile way to stir up a revolution which should inflict on the Turk such a blow as the Armenians in Russian Caucasus inflicted on the Tatar 15 years ago, but most of the Armenians were quiet enough and only wanted to be left alone. Moreover there was a strong party which was definitely hostile to the revolutionaries and looked for the prosperity and happiness of the Armenians in an *entente* with the Turks.

One other province of Anatolia may be dealt with here, not because it is a part of Kurdistan, but because it once belonged to Armenia. When in the 12th century of our era the Seljuks put an end to the Armenian power in Kurdistan, a relative of the murdered ruler of Ani founded in Cilicia the kingdom of Lesser Armenia. It lasted little over two hundred years, when it was overthrown by the Mamluks, but it left its trace in innumerable ruins of fine stone built churches, and in a large Armenian population. This community suffered terrible things in the massacres of 1909, but was saved from complete destruction, largely owing to the intervention of a British Officer, at that time Consul at Adana. The saviour and those whom he preserved have alike perished. He rests in honour on a headland in Gallipoli and the Armenians of Cilicia have been put to the sword at the order of Turk and German.

I recall, in vivid contrast to what is, thank God, the British temper, a story for the truth of which I can answer though it has not hitherto been published. At the outbreak of the massacres a small party of German Engineers were engaged in survey work for the railway at Baghcheh on the pass over Anti-Taurus. The party consisted of some four or five men, and with them was a girl, the daughter of the chief surveyor. Baghcheh is a village which was partly peopled by Armenians, a number of whom took shelter in the wooden house occupied by the Germans. The Kurds assembled round it, crying out that they would set it on fire if the refugees were not delivered to them. It was possible, though not probable, that the threat might have been put into execution, but the Germans took no risk. They opened their doors and thrust out the helpless people who were murdered before their eyes. A few days later they fled down to Adana, under an escort sent out by the British Consul. They passed by Osmaniyah, at the foot of the hills, where an English traveller, who had turned the Khan in which he found himself into a hospital and sanctuary for wounded Armenians, saw them and was astounded at the ignoble terror which they exhibited. To him they gave the presence of the girl as excuse for their action ; let those accept it who will.

Socially Cilicia has usually belonged rather to Syria than to Asia Minor, from which it is separated geographically by the high range of Taurus. The wealth of the Adana plain, watered by three great rivers, has defied the ravages of many invading armies and under a civilized administration would develop into boundless prosperity. An old established railway, originally built by the French, connects Adana with Tarsus and the port of Marsina, and the Baghdad railway traverses the western half of the province from the Cilician Gates to the Amanus. Roads there are none worthy of the name, except the highway which preceded the Baghdad line. The rivers have been bridged from ancient date to give it passage. The Cydnus is still spanned by a bridge which goes back to the Amenian kingdom, the Sarus by a bridge of Justinian's and the Pyramus by a bridge dating from the time of Constantius. The population, even for Turkish Asia, is bewilderingly varied and receives in winter an influx of Circassians, Kurds and Turanian tribes from the mountain ranges. There is small hope of peace and security unless the Government of this distracted country is taken for ever out of Ottoman hands.

Turkish Provinces —The Anatolian Plateau.

THE centre of Asia Minor is occupied by a vast upland, over 3,000 ft. above sea level, stretching some 400 miles from Afium Qarah Hissar on the west to Caesarea on the east, and 300 miles or more from Angora on the north to the slopes of Taurus on the south. This region has so distinctive a character that in any description of Anatolia it must claim a separate place. It is inhabited very largely by men of Turanian race. It was the centre of the Seljuq empire of Rum which at the close of the 11th century established its seat at Konia, and it abounds in magnificent Seljuq monuments. Half-nomadic Turkish tribes, Turkoman and Yuruk, people the country districts, but in the towns, besides the Turkish element, there are—or were —large colonies of Armenians, and near Konia there are villages entirely Greek, though until recently when a marked tendency to revive the Greek tongue overtook the Greek subjects of the Porte, no language but Turkish was known to their inhabitants.

I have approached the plateau from almost all points of the compass, but from no direction is it more impressive than from the west. You leave behind you a land of lakes and running water, a land which, as I shall presently describe, seems to the European more Occidental than Oriental, and crossing the last pass over Murad Dagh or Sultan Dagh, turn from what is in spirit Europe to what is in spirit as well as in fact Asia. I cannot otherwise qualify the distinction between the two continents than by saying that in Europe and in the western coast lands of the Levant which appertain if not geographically, yet by virtue of their characteristics to Europe, nature seems willing to lend herself to the purposes of mankind, obedient to his moulding hand; whereas in Asia man makes complete submission, nests himself where he can between inaccessible mountains and inhospitable deserts, drinks of bitter inland waters, and where the soil chooses to give in abundance, toils beneath a scorching sun or freezes in the rigours of a formidable cold. To these conditions the Anatolion plateau is, as it were, the introduction. On its wide surface there is neither refuge nor shelter, save where an abrupt volcanic outcrop such as the Qarah Dagh, the Qarajah Dagh, Hasan Dagh, or Mount Argaeus over against Caesarea, gathers and preserves the winter snows to deck its slopes in vegetation, and protects village and croft within its folds.

To the north of the road from Ak Sarai to Konia a salt lake covers many miles of the plateau and the surrounding country is pitiless wilderness, producing nothing but a sparse growth of acrid plants on which no animal can pasture ; but in the west, round Konia and south to Karaman, there are thousands of acres of corn land. When I was last in Konia the scheme for bringing water to the plain from Lake Bay Shehr was about to be undertaken and I believe it was executed before the outbreak of the war. It will assure the harvests even in dry seasons and make the fortune of the Circassian villages below Qarah Dagh. Here, too, the Circassians have had a hard struggle to live, not so much because of local hostility as on account of official neglect and an entire lack of provision for their settlement. I have seen troops of Muhajir —for, undeterred, they are still coming in from the Caucasus—who have been kept waiting for a year or more in Konia before land was allotted to them. Having no means of subsistence they were obliged to kill the cattle they had brought with them and sell their household goods, and when at last they entered into possession of a corner of the arid plain, they had neither animals to stock their farms nor furnishings for the mud cottages which they set themselves to build. It was not, therefore, a matter for surprise if their villages presented a singularly poverty-stricken appearance.

Under the hills there is always cultivation; the Yuruks find in them pasturage for their flocks and the Turkomans go up in summer to their Yailahs. The north-east flanks of Hasan Dagh are a marvel of beauty and luxuriance, and Mount Argaeus is famous for its vineyards and fruit trees. There the volcanic soil is eminently well adapted to the culture of the vine and the vintages might water into successful rivalry with those of Veravius and Etna. To the archæologist the mountains offer sites of the deepest interest. I found a Hittite High Place on the top of Qarah Dagh, together with the ruins of a tiny and very ancient church and tomb which had sanctified to the later faith a spot venerated from the beginning of historic time by the inhabitants of the plateau. Ruined churches and monasteries crown the summit of the Qarajah Dagh and are scattered over the upper slopes of Hasan Dagh, while on Mount Argaeus the rock cut cells of anchorites exist up to the snow line and even above it.

The modern fame of the Konia plain is due
mainly to its intimate connection with the Baghdad
railway project, but the Baghdad line is not the
only, nor was it the first means of access by rail
to the plateau. The history of the three railways
constructed from the coast to the high inland
plains, only two of which attained their goal, is
so significant politically and economically that it
merits careful attention. The natural outlet by
which Anatolian products would make their way
to the markets of Europe is not Constantinople
but Smyrna, and the first lines to the interior were
begun from that port. The Smyrna-Kassaba
railway, directed by a French company (it was in
origin a British enterprize) followed the valley of
the Hermus and was extended to Afium Qarah
Hissar, while the Aidin line, at the outbreak of war
still in British hands, was constructed along the
yet richer valley of the Macander. This last is
financially the soundest and most remunerative
of any of the Anatolian railways, not excepting
that which runs from Haidar Pasha to Angora.
Since it was from the first entirely unassisted by
a kilometric guarantee, it was essential to adopt
measures which should assure its success on ordinary business principles. Accordingly it was not

pushed through hastily from its base to a remote point in the interior, but allowed to develop slowly, each section paying its way as it advanced by means of short branch lines which tapped the fertile country on either side. There was always the intention of carrying it through ultimately to Konia, and if this had been done, it would have ended by becoming commercially the most flourishing railway in Turkey, but while railhead yet rested at Dinair, east of Aidin, the Baghdad railway project, primarily not economic but strategic, took form, and the influence of the German company was devoted to the hindering of so obviously dangerous a competitor. With considerable difficulty the British company obtained the concession for an extension from Dinair to Lake Egirdir, and the section was completed before the war, but whether the Germans would have permitted the linking up of Egirdir with Konia, which would have been so clearly advantageous to the country and might well have diverted the products of the interior from Constantinople to Smyrna, is a question concerning which we need not now hazard a solution. The Smyrna-Kassaba line, not quite so prudently developed as the Aidin, nor able to dispense with a kilometric guarantee, had reached the plateau

at Afium before the Baghdad railway concession
to the Germans was completed. It was, however,
effectively prevented from playing what should
have been its natural part as an outlet from the
plateau to the Mediterranean by the simple
process of forbidding it to join up with the Con-
stantinople-Konia line. The few hundred yards'
gap between the French and the German stations,
necessitating the breaking of bulk for all goods
coming up from the south, to a great extent
deterred exporters from sending their merchandize
(chiefly grain) to Symrna, as they would usually
have preferred to do if transport facilities had
been equal ; and for my part I never passed
through Afium without reflecting upon the
economic crime which the German conces-
sionnaires were committing in preventing
commerce from taking its cheapest route to the
markets of Europe.

The Baghdad railway concession was, as every
one knows, obtained by the Emperor William in
person when he visited Constantinople in 1898.
It was a *quid pro quo*, he having resolutely an-
nounced his intention of backing the Sultan, who
was then somewhat ill-regarded by the rest of
Christendom, owing to the active part he had played

during 1896-7 in urging his Moslem subjects to massacre the Armenians under his rule. The scheme took the shape of a colossal extension to a second railway which had already reached the plateau from the coast, namely the Haidar Pasha line. From small beginnings—it had grown out of a local railway built by a British company between Constantinople, or rather Haidar Pasha, and Ismid— this line had become an important means of communication, reaching to Eskisheher and Angora. It had lost in the process its British character and assumed one which was wholly German. It tapped the rich agricultural country south of the Sea of Marmora, so far as a single line without branch feeders could fulfil that purpose, and from Eskisheher to Angora served a very fertile district. Before the outbreak of the war, it had dispensed with the kilometric guarantee which had originally been assigned to it. Very different was the position with regard to the extension to Konia and then to the Taurus which was completed in 1906. Without the Bey Shehr irrigation scheme there was no probability that this section would be able to pay its way, and even if that scheme were carried out, it was likely that many years would elapse before the Konia line ceased to be a charge upon

the Ottoman taxpayer. But since the two lines
from Smyrna were, as has been explained, blocked
by the jealousy of the Germans, it was impossible
to develop the Konia plain except by the Haidar
Pasha route, and even if the Baghdad railway, with
its unprecedented guarantee, drew heavily upon the
narrow resources of the Turkish exchequer, there
can be no doubt that it benefited the western parts
of the plateau. Up to the foot of Taurus, therefore, it may fairly be regarded as a commercial
enterprize, but its continuation over Taurus had
no connection with economics. A port on the
Sea of Marmora was not calculated to attract
the products of Cilicia, North Syria and
Northern Mesopotamia from their natural outlets
at Mersina and Alexandretta, and though evry
much can be said in favour of opening up the
cornlands east of Aleppo, as well as those which
lie on the other side of Euphrates, and rendering
them accessible by rail from Alexandretta, this
was in fact an afterthought and not part of the
original design. But the costly work of tunnelling
the Taurus and Amanus was not and could not
have been undertaken with any economic end in
view. The idea of linking Baghdad with Constantinople fell in with 'Abdul Hamid's policy of

centralization, which in a country like Turkey was
as dangerous a conception as any which could
have been entertained ; and after 'Abdul Hamid's
fall, when the unhappy conglomerate which has
been known as the Ottoman Empire fell into the
hands of politicians yet more insanely bent then
he on drawing all authority into the Turkish
net at Constantinople, the completion of the
Baghdad railway was yet more eagerly desired.
In the eyes of the Committee of Union and Progress the creation of a potent Turkey, a power
which should take its place among War Lords,
demanded not the pacification of the races subject to the Porte by a wise and liberal consideration
of their grievances, but political anihilation which
should silence those who ventured to have grievances. The first essential was the opening up of the
empire by strategic railways so as to permit the
quick passage of troops from one point to another.
The trunk line policy was no less in tune with
German ambitions. Turkey appeared as the long
dreamed of place in the Sun, Berlin to Baghdad
was a cry which would have won an election, if
German rulers had been dependent upon the wishes
of an electorate, and the hopes which were aroused
were given additional radiance by the reflection.

that success implied the ousting of British influence and British enterprize, and the establishing in Western Asia of a menacing counter-weight to British domination in India and in Egypt. Nor do I feel a shadow of doubt that but for the outbreak of war in 1914 these aims would have been realized, unless the growth of an effective Slav Power in the Balkans should have interposed an impermeable, if not an actively hostile entity between Central Europe and Constantinople. It was this danger, a danger created by the Balkan war of 1912-13, which precipitated the decision by arms long regarded by Germany unavoidable.

From the briefest survey of the history of Turkish railway construction one salient principle can be deduced for future guidance. It is that a prolonged and naked trunk line, linking up provinces which have no essential economic connection, has many grave drawbacks. It entails a heavy kilometric guarantee, that is to say a charge on the taxpayer from which he does not derive commensurate profit, and it tends to induce a windy impression of unity among peoples who are not yet ready for any very closely knit, not to say centralized, administration, as well as vain talk among half-baked statesmen, native and foreign,

Far sounder, politically as well as economically, are the rules which guided the constructors of the Aidin line. Following their example, it will be well to take railway development in Turkish Asia by sections, allowing the various ports, whether on the Persian Gulf or on the Mediterranean or the Black Sea, to push out feelers into the regions which they command; letting extension to hand in hand with an industrial and agricultural progress which shall provide every additional mile of rail with the prospect of a satisfactory balance sheet.

Though the agricultural products of the Turkish as well as of the Arab provinces will no doubt continue to be of paramount importance, it will not be long, if circumstances are favourable, before the development of mineral resources begins to play a part, especially in the Turkish provinces. The mineral wealth of Anatolia is considerable. It has scarcely, as yet, been exploited, or if exploited at all the methods employed have been almost ludicrously inadequate. I have in mind the valuable copper mines of Arghanah, in the mountains between Kharput and Biyarbakr, where after a rude process of smelting, the metal is run into

circular moulds and the resulting disks, two to a
camel load, are borne over the hills by interminable slow-footed caravans—surely the most improbable means of access to a manufacturing district
(if I may so call the wild Arghanah valley) which
you might be privileged to see. The saltpetre of
Qaisariyah, the argentiferous lead of Keban
Nadan, the coal, iron, mercury and zinc which
are known to exist in the Anatolian highlands,
the immense salt deposits of the plains await
capital and means of transport for their successful
exploitation.

Though I began by saying that the Anatolian
plateau was a region apart, I have been led, in
describing it, into topics which concern the Ottoman empire as a whole, but this divergence is
not illogical. The plateau is the heart of Turkey.
Across it from east to west lie the great roads which
have from time immemorial connected the Mediterranean coast with interior Asia, and from north
to south the few and difficult tracks which have
been the way of armies rather than of merchants.
Chief among these last, and indeed almost the only
north and south road of historic interest, is that

which crosses Taurus by the Cilicians Gates, the route followed by the Baghdad railway which has been of such sinister import to the Ottoman empire. And this road (for it is not yet wholly rail) is serving to-day, as it served in the past, not the beneficent purposes of peace but the ruinous demands of war

Turkish Provinces—The Anatolian Coast.

WHEN to the session of thought I summon recollection of the coast lands of Asia Minor, the enchantment of those radiant shores and exquisite valleys seems to outstrip reality. The furnace heat and burning winds of a Mesopotamian July, the dust which envelopes life and calls it before its time to mingle with the ultimate element of its composition, enhance remembered beauties ; but they need no such sharp edge of comparison. Not only do the coast lands satisfy the physical eye, but they fill the imagination with the rumour of legend and the echo of history. History and legend are alike Greek, or they have come to us through a Greek interpretation, for it was here that Greece took her widest expansion and developed her latest civilization. Famous settlements like Miletus and Ephesus rivalled Athens and Sparta in their prime, and after European Greece had ceased to play a dominant part, Asiatic Greece continued to mould the life and thought of mankind. Asia Minor transmitted to the infant state of Rome her quota of the mysticism as well as the sensuality of half-Hellenized oriental cults, and in the plastic arts set forth human emotion as it had never before been portrayed with the idealized passion of the school of Pergamon.

The land is full of Greek towns, splendid still in ruin. Some have made their final contribution to history and to art at the bidding of the Austrian, and more completely, of the German excavator. Honour where honour is due : let it be given therefore to the Germans at Magnesia, Priene (loveliest of excavated cities), Miletus, Didymus and Pergamon, and to the Austrians at Ephesus. Other Hellenistic sites are still veiled in "forest branches and the trodden weed." So Aphrodisias, Sagalassos on its hill top, and a score of ruin fields by the sea remain half buried, and as you ride through wooded hills you will come unexpectedly upon the white columns of a temple, like that of Euromos near Milas, dropping shaft by shaft into unheeded oblivion. The air is full of Greek mythology. Oenone cries through the forests of the Bithynian Olympus, Endymion is held in death-like sleep on Lotmos, Marsyas, hanging from the Phrygian three, expiates his triumph over Apollo. Look where you will, all the Anatolian myths are tinged with the sorrowfulness of Asia, being born of Asia and cast by the Greek mind into perfection of melancholy form.

If you turn from the ghost of a pàst civilization and look upon the country as it now lives, the Hellenic element in the coast districts still plays an important part. The population of Asia Minor is at a rough estimate some nine million souls, of whom but a million are Greeks ; since however these last are mainly concentrated in the ports or not far from them, they bulk large in this particular region. More than half the inhabitants of Smyrna, for example, are Greek. They control the inland trade, though the Armenians have offered them strenuous and increasingly successful rivalry, and as far east as Egirdir are an invariable item in the commercial population of the towns. Another and less meritorious renown was theirs. The brigandage which was rampant round Smyrna and in the ranges which separate the Hermus from the Masander valley was attributable to Greek bands. Some of the leaders had a local fame comparable only to that of a Robin Hood or a Dick Turpin. There was one Chekirji who in the decade before the war terrorized the whole country and provided it

with endless store of romantic tales. At the last
the Turkish gendarmerie succeeded in cornering
him—this was if I remember rightly in 1913—and
obtained possession of a headless body which was
identified as his. Men said that he had died by
his own hand rather than suffer capture, but that
his followers had made their escape carrying with
them his head, in the hope that the Government
would remain in ignorance of his fate. Why it
was that robber bands continued to flourish can
be elucidated partly by an incident which I witnessed. It was in the days of Chekirj and I
was riding up from Halicarnassus to Aidin, not
far from the Tmolus massif which the robber
chief held in undisputed possession. I travelled
quickly, very lightly laden, one servant and a
pack mule forming my party. At night we
lodged in the guest chamber of some hospitable
elder of the village where we halted. So by
stream and pasture we came to Ileina a day's
ride south of Aidin, and put up in the house of
an Agha. There we met a Turkish Officer of
gendarmerie who was out brigand hunting, and
with him in the evening I had much friendly
talk. That very night his men caught a brigand
who was brought in to the Agha's house armed

to the teeth and presenting an appearance in all ways suited to his calling. Moreover he was identified by the officer, who referred for the purpose to an official Who's Who of brigands which he carried with him. It contained personal descriptions of noted outlaws and to one of these our friend corresponded exactly. Amid excited congratulations he was placed in confinement, I think it was in the cow-shed that he was imprisoned. But his detention lasted no longer than a night. Next day he bribed successfully the Agha and the officer and obtained a surreptitious release, of which the news was brought to me while I was examining the ruins of a temple of Hecate hard by. It must be borne in mind that the officer had to live and that his pay was months in arrears. This incident made me understand better than before the difficulties experienced by the Ottoman Government in suppressing brigandage.

So much for the Greeks, not wholly a desirable element. Like the Armenians they were regarded by the Turks with jealous eyes because the slower-witted Ottoman could not compete with them in commerce. Here, as elsewhere, hewers of wood and drawers of water—there is an interesting

group expressly known as Tahtaji, woodmen—
the Turanian was at his best in the country districts, as a peasant uncomplainingly tilling the
soil of which the rich returns were reft from him
by official extortion, by floods which the local
Qaimmaqam had neglected to restrain, or by the
vicissitudes of transport over unmetalled road
and unbridged stream. The Mæander valley
suffered heavily from the depredations of its
river. I have seen the water three miles wide
near its mouth at Miletus, and have splashed for
an hour through flooded fields south of Aidin.
It was the peasantry of Asia Minor which bore the
brunt of the Balkan War of 1912-13. Depleted
by battle and disease in those years, it has been
called on since the autumn of 1914 to fight for
Germany in Europe, in the Caucasus and in the
plains of Mesopotamia. Its numbers must by
now have suffered such reduction that it is difficult to imagine how the fields are ploughed and
the crops saved. Even as I knew the Anatolian
Coast, indigenous labour was insufficient for
agricultural needs and every summer it was
supplemented by an influx of Albanians to gather
the harvest. The commercial population has
been devastated by other causes. On the coast

the Greeks have been driven from their homes to herd and starve in the interior, and the Armenians must have gone under. The condition of the Anatolian coast lands can be only less lamentable than that of Syria.

I have spoken mainly of the western fringe of Asia Minor because it is the part which I know best, but the lands bordering the Sea of Marmora and the Black Sea are no less fruitful. From the headland of Troy past Brussa to Isnik, the ancient Nicaea, from Insik to Ismid and east to Kastamuni there are fertile belts of cultivation extending over the plains and following the windings of the valleys. Some of this region falls within the orbit of tourists, and for one who has visited Konia or Aidin there must be many hundreds who know the matchless plain of Brussa and have ridden across to Nicaea to join the railway at Ismid. Brussa like Konia was a capital, not of Seljuks but of the Ottomans themselves, for over a hundred years before they wrested Constantinople from the Byzantine. It may— who knows ?—be an Ottoman capital once more.

Very different are the southern shores of Asia Minor from Halicarnassus, the modern Budrum, to the Cilician border. The Taurus range drops so steeply to the sea that there is often no possible road along the shore, and the ruins of Hellenistic cities which adorned Lycia and Pamphylia must be approached by water. The best means of access to the interior has always been from Adalia whence a road leads over a high pass to Lake Buldur, a little to the west of Egirdir. The ruins of Sagalassos stand near the top of the pass—I was once there late in April and saw the theatre still half full of snow. This ancient channel of commerce was about to be developed before the war by the Italian Government, which had obtained a concession for the building of a railway from Adalia to Buldur where it would have linked up with the Egirdir extension of our Aidin line. One of the assets of the southern slope of Taurus, both here and in Cilicia, is timber. The afforestation is capable of great improvement, and in Asiatic Turkey where scientific woodmanship is unknown and the trees, nibbled by goats and lopped by charcoal burners, are seldom allowed to reach any reasonable size, properly controlled forests would be of the highest value.

Besides the main railways from Symrna to the interior, of which I have already spoken, there

were two other short lines from the coast. The
few miles of railway from Mudania on the Black
Sea to Brussa have been in existence for 15 years
or more, and just before the war an extension was
opened of the Manissa-Soma line, itself a branch
of the Smyrna-Kassaba. This extension runs to
Panderma, on the Sea of Marmora west of Mudania,
and thus connects the Mediterranean port of
Smyrna with a port on the inland waters of Marmora. To go by rail from Smyrna to Constantinople was a four days' journey, *via* Afium,
Eskisheher and Ismid.

A branch from the Aidin line to Sokia, one of
the centres of the liquorice trades reaches almost
to the southern coast, for Sokia is not far from the
mouth of the Macander ; but west of the Baghdad railway there is no north and south line
across Asia Minor, nor do the trade routes lie
in that direction. Except for small, self-contained
districts like the Brussa plain, the tendency of
trade over western Asia Minor is to drain down to
Smyrna, where it has access to an open sea.

I have come to the end. The next stop would
take me out of Asiatic Turkey to Gallipoli, sown
with our dead, to Constantinople, where the evil

counsels of the Committee and the German still guide the Ottoman Empire on the path to ruin. If I were to set myself to make a brief for the Turk I should not be without arguments. No one who knows him and his history can accuse him of having been the sole agent of destruction in the lands he governed. A heavy burden of blame lies upon the nations of Europe, for whom Turkey has been a pawn in an age-long and shameful game of jealous cupidity. But the time for such pleas is past. It has been blotted out by the blood and tears of the subject races. *Venit summa dies et ineluctabile tempus*—let us consider what the new day should bring.

I take it for granted that the Arab provinces cannot be allowed to remain under Turkish rule, nor yet the mountain districts, including Cilicia which on three separate occasions during the past 20 years have been thrown, by order from Constantinople, into the worst horrors or religious strife. Where Ottoman sovereignty is preserved either the Christian population must be helped to withdraw, or there must be a binding pledge— binding on Europe as well as on Turkey—that they shall not be molested. Even if we leave out of

count the wheat-growing area of the plateau and
the richly varied fertility of the coast lands—
though we may be certain that they will not be left
undeveloped—what will be the results of pacification and progress over Asiatic Turkey ? We are
dealing with one of the most important agricultural
areas in the world. The 'Iraq alone is not second
in productiveness to Egypt, while in acreage it
is more than twice as large the Syrian granaries,
without modern facilities of transport, helped to
feed Rome, and the commerce of the ancient as
well as of the mediæval world flowed of necessity
to eastern industrial centres. The maritime city
states of Italy, Genoa and Venice, owed their
prosperity to Oriental trade, and the ports of the
Adriatic profited by it in a similar measure. Not
long after the final decline of the Abbasid and the
Byzontine empires came the discovery of America
and the opening up of fresh trade routes across the
Atlantic. The rehabilitation of the Near East may
once more alter the balance or let us say establish
a just balance, by recreating a market which has
been for centuries in abeyance. It will add immea-
surably to the wealth of a universe wasted by war
and provide new fields for the reviving industries

of Europe. And since all successful commerce must be equally beneficial to both parties concerned (for in trade there is no good bargain except that from which both the contractors profit) East and West will once more be linked together by common advantage.

MIDDLE EASTERN WOMEN AND HISTORICAL HORIZONS

Paul Rich

Gertrude Bell's life is is a reminder of how misleading one of the favourite myths about women's place in history is - that of the idle gentlelady. Patricia Branca in an essay "Image and Reality" describes the entrenched standard plot in historiography: "According to this view, middle-class parents, in their desire to imitate the upper classes, sent their daughters off to boarding schools where they were to acquire the elegant accomplishments necessary to becoming the 'perfect lady': a little French, some music, some dancing, the art of fancy needlework, and, of course, all the rules of improper etiquette."[1] In actual fact, even if they did receive instruction in needlework, women of Bell's era often managed in the face of incredible prejudice - as did Bell - to show just how able they really were.

If the historical misconceptions about English women are numerous, the distortions about Arab women are legend. Whether Western or Arab, women are the Middle East's forgotten story. (See *Arab Girl Labourers in Baghdad*.) The suppression of women's historical status in the Middle East parallels the actual suppression to which they have been subjected, their identity not so much forgotten as never recognised. Little has changed for women in recent decades; if anything the restrictions on their lives have been tightened: "...in the Islamic world today, and among Islamic minorities in the west," writes the Muslim journalist Fadia Faqir, "there is what Salman Rushdie has described as 'Already Existing Islam', with 'granite, heartless certainties', stifling Muslim societies. Between us and Allah stand the self-appointed clerics who claim to be the sole defenders of the Islamic faith, and who use 'holier inist and novelist Nawal El Saadawi comments on the role that Arab historians have had in this:

> "Just as the historical and social consciousness of women has been distorted through the falsification of history, so has their consciousness of self been warped by a spurious glorification of the past. A conflict has been created between the concept of the authentic Arab personality or identity and a modern cultural consciousness based on knowledge and rational intelligence."[3]

She adds sardonically:

> "Heritage is a tool which all present political forces use according to their interests and their perspectives."[4]

By making the position of women a matter of sharaf and insisting that women's affairs must be masturah (chaste and hidden), Middle Eastern society has made imprisonment and banning the reward for historical truthfulness.[5]

Unquestionably a great deal of the work of Arab historians has gone out of its way to perpetuate debilitating notions of the innately inferior characteristics of women, their unsuitability as professionals and the religious merits of their mute confinement to the house as childbearers and domestics. Discriminations, including restrictions on education and prohibitions against such simple exercises as driving a car or shopping unaccompanied by a man, are explained as solicitude. Man-made restrictions are presented as God-given precepts.

ARAB GIRL LABOURERS.

Although the history of the struggle of women in the Middle East for basic rights cannot be separated from that of the general women's movement, it has special nuances. The veil is symbolic of all the entrenched peculiarities which are associated with a culture confused by theological claims and particularly plagued by patriarchy. A number of Allborough books address these issues.

Foremost perhaps is the autobiography of Selma Ekrem, *Unveiled*, in iUniverse.com Middle East Lives series. Born into an aristocratic and Europeanised Ottoman family -- her father was secretary to the Sultan -- Selma Ekrem was a brilliantly critical but good-humoured observer of court life in the very end days of the Turkish Empire. When her father became Governor of Jerusalem, she accompanied him and was able to write about Palestine just before World War I. Ultimately the hypocrisy of orthodox Islam's treatment of women caused her to flee to the United States, although she finally returned to play a part in the modernising of post-war Turkey. The number of Muslim women forced to flee to the West in order to teach and write without censorship is enough to justify a full-length study, long overdue.

Another book of considerable relevance is *By Tigris and Euphrates* by E.S.Stevens, published in the Allborough Middle East Studies series as Devil-Worship in Iraq. E.S.Stevens was the Lady Drower, whose exploits as a journalist during the Iraqi civil war in the early 1920s were rather out of keeping with jealous preconceptions of the behaviour of the daughter of an Anglican cleric. Honoured by Uppsala and Oxford with doctorates but now largely forgotten, she is another woman of the Middle East who deserves renewed recognition.

Similarly, the Middle East Classics include Eleanor Egan's *War in the Cradle of the Gulf*, published in a new edition as *Wartime in Baghdad*. Egan was a well-connected American journalist who ingeniously managed to tour the warfront between the British and the Turks at the height of hostilities. Women expatriates such as Stevens and Egan who were able to travel in an area where the hardiest of men feared for survival constitute a unique class of witnesses. Although usually less exciting, the challenges to women pursuing careers today are not completely different from those facing their sisters in the Victorian and Edwardian eras. The commonalities through the decades have attracted the attention of Professor Judith Bennett, who writes:

> By advocating generalisation, I do not mean to suggest that we should ignore differences in women's lives, differences related to class, race, sexuality, and the like. Indeed, once we risk generalization, distinctions within broad trends will be absolutely crucial to our understanding of historical patriarchy...We haven't yet looked hard enough at patriarchies *as patriarchies* to be able to reach many firm conclusions. But our tasks are clear; we must historicize patriarchy not only by identifying its main mechanisms (both those specific to only a few societies and those common to most) but also by examining it has managed to survive and endure.[7]

The influence of women in the Middle East, and the consequences of the severe repression to which they have been subjected, so far has only received token historical attention. The reworking of the record will perhaps be assisted by the publication of more texts by women writers, such as those in the Allborough list. What is owed is not sympathy but simple justice.

An increasingly important clearing house for information about women in the Middle East is the Association for Middle East Women's studies, which can be reached at 64 Alumni Avenue, Providence, Rhode Island 02906. The Association is an affiliate of the Middle East Studies Association and has published *Women in the Muslim World, A Bibliography of Books and Articles primarily in the English*

WOMEN IN BAGHDAD

Language. Meeting needs in this long neglected area, the 'Amnews' - in addition to an annual conference with appropriate papers - publish a newsletter which includes a strong review section. Panels at recent meetings have considered such topics as "Sensuality in the Rural Society of late-Ottoman Transjordan", "Love and Power in Arab Brother/Sister Relationships", "Gender as Seen Through Children's Eyes in Modern Arabic Literature", "Arabic Narrative Discourse and Sexual Politics", and "The Feminization of Difference: Imaging the Arab Woman".

Of equal helpfulness in raising consciousness about such issues is the women's studies section of the American Historical Association (an association which of course is concerned with history worldwide, in contrast with the more American-centred Organization of American Historians), and a similar section of the Modern Language Association.

A number of prospective titles in the various iUniverse.com Middle East series have been selected in the hopes of making a contribution to the rapidly growing field of women's studies and will be of interest to anyone aware of past omissions in this area. A problem that hopefully will be discussed as the various series progress is one that has not been considered enough: the actual authorship of many standard works about the Middle East. There is little mention by bibliographers of the distortions in presenting books as the sole work of male authors which may upon examination prove to have been the team effort of a man and woman or actually the work of an anonymous woman whose contributions were concealed. In the next few decades a number of important Middle East titles attributed to men may be found to be collaborative efforts or actually written almost totally by their anonymous female 'helpmates'.

Nothing would please the editor more than to be able to present evidence of such authorship and correspondence on the topic may be addressed to him at The Hoover Institution, Stanford, California. We are a long way from achieving an egalitarian and androgynous society, but surely history has a part to be played.

(See *A Syrian Gentlewoman* and *A Christian Girl*, Bagh-dad from Robert Casey's *Baghdad & Points East*.)

NOTES

1. Patricia Branca, "Image and Reality: The Myth of the Idle Victorian Woman", Hary S.Hartman and Lois Banner eds., *Clio's Consciousness Raised: New Perspectives on the History of Women*, Harper & Row, New York, 1974, 180.

2. Fadia Faqir, "Unveiling Paradise", *New Statesman & Society*, 14 February 1991, 12.

3. Nawal El Saadawi, "The Political Challenges Facing Arab Women at the End of the 20th Century", Nahid Tou-bia ed., *Women of the Arab World: The Coming Challenge*, Zed Books, London and New Jersey, 1988, 21.

4. *Ibid*.

5. Faqir, "Unveiling Paradise", 12.

6. Fatima El Mernissi, "Democracy as Moral Distintegra-tion: The Contradiction between Religious Belief and Citi-zenship as a Manifestation of the History of the Arab Identity", Toubia ed., *Women of the Arab World*, 36

7. Judith H.Bennett, "Feminism and History", *Gender & History*, Vol.1 No.3, Autumn 1989, 266.

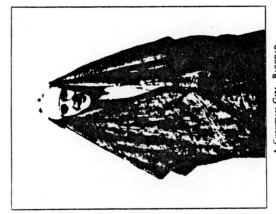

A Christian Girl, Baghdad

A Syrian Gentlewoman

Printed in the United States
792400001B